1 MONTH OF
FREE
READING

at
www.ForgottenBooks.com

By purchasing this book you are eligible for one month membership to ForgottenBooks.com, giving you unlimited access to our entire collection of over 1,000,000 titles via our web site and mobile apps.

To claim your free month visit:

www.forgottenbooks.com/free821693

ISBN 978-0-365-00822-4
PIBN 10821693

For support please visit www.forgottenbooks.com

MADE AND PRINTED IN GREAT BRITAIN BY
MORRISON AND GIBB LIMITED
FOR
T. & T. CLARK, EDINBURGH
LONDON : SIMPKIN, MARSHALL, HAMILTON, KENT, AND CO. LIMITED
NEW YORK : CHARLES SCRIBNER'S SONS

THE
SEMITIC RELIGIONS

HEBREW, JEWISH, CHRISTIAN, MOSLEM

THE TWENTY-SECOND SERIES OF
CROALL LECTURES

BY

DAVID M. KAY, D.S.O., D.D.

REGIUS PROFESSOR OF HEBREW AND ORIENTAL LANGUAGES
IN ST. MARY'S COLLEGE, UNIVERSITY OF ST. ANDREWS

Edinburgh : T. & T. CLARK, 38 George Street
1923

WITH REVERENT GRATITUDE

TO THE FOUNDER

OF THE LECTURESHIP

JOHN CROALL

D. M. K.

PREFACE

JOHN CROALL, Esq., of Southfield, being "deeply interested in the defence and maintenance of the doctrines of the Christian Religion, and desirous of increasing the religious literature of Scotland," instituted a Lectureship. The Lectures "shall be delivered biennially in Edinburgh," "shall be not less than six in number," and shall be devoted to a consideration of the Evidences of Natural and Revealed Religion and the Doctrines of the Christian Religion.

These six Lectures on " The Semitic Religions " were delivered in the Moray Aisle of St. Giles' Cathedral, Edinburgh, on alternate Sundays between January 28 and April 8, 1923. The Lecturer gratefully acknowledges his obligation to the Very Rev. A. Wallace Williamson, C.V.O., D.D., and the Kirk Session for permission to deliver the Lectures in St. Giles.

D. M. KAY.

April 9, 1923.

CONTENTS

THE SEMITIC RELIGIONS

LECTURE I.

HEBREW RELIGION—PRIMITIVE AND PROPHETIC.

History. IT is now fully five thousand years since the human race awoke from its aboriginal slumbers and began to take an interest in itself and the world. These fifty or sixty centuries afford records, scanty at first, which furnish contemporary evidence of the events they describe. But men existed long before they could read or write. The invention of writing, syllabic or alphabetic, the art of suggesting to the eye the speech which primarily was meant for the ear, was a difficult achievement. More than half the race is still illiterate; and the independent formation of a new script has been exceptional, even among talented races. Five thousand years ago, the inhabitants of the earth had neither the power nor the desire to write a history of their proceedings. Their motive in making records was to fix a bargain or treaty, to enforce a law, to celebrate a victory, or to mark a building.   The curiosity of remote descendants was little considered ; the fear of future oblivion was not so patent as the satisfaction that something exceptional had been accomplished.

What preceded history ? When we go beyond the province of that history, which is attested by human documents, definitely located in time and place and intelligibly connected with the ascertained sequence of events, can we form any estimate of man and his religion, especially of the antecedents of Biblical religion ?   Dr. Johnson, speaking in no very sympathetic way of " antiquarian research," declared that " all that is really known of the ancient state of Britain is contained in a few pages.   We *can* know no more than what the old writers have told us." There seemed at that time little hope of getting beyond the common story of the world's beginning. The book of Genesis was then the one sole voice from a vanished world.   Greece and Rome had no clear history going back beyond seven or eight centuries before the Christian era ;   and even that short period had a perplexing intermixture of fable and legend.   Egypt was full of mysterious monuments, but nobody knew whether the hieroglyphic symbols were real writing or

fantastic ornament. Babylon was a graveyard
of empires, silent and forsaken, in accordance
with the doom of the prophets. For fifteen
hundred years before the foundation of Rome
(753 B.C.) and the first Greek Olympiad (776 B.C.)
the only source of information was the Old
Testament. It stood alone, detached from all
secular annals, seeming like a voice from heaven.
Its singular authority arose from a certain inherent
dignity as well as from its uniqueness. The best
minds made but little effort to extend their
horizons beyond the Bible in narrating the
history of the world.

Unwritten history as conceived a century ago. The prevalence of this Biblical representation of early history may be illustrated from the seventh edition of the
Encyclopædia Britannica, which was completed
about 1840. The articles concerned with primitive
antiquity are still hampered by the chronology
of Archbishop Ussher (died 1656). After careful
computations, Ussher had established a maximum
of four thousand and four years as the utmost
limit of time for all that had happened previous
to the Christian Era. The writer on Egypt
says : " The reign of Menes forms the extreme
limit of legitimate curiosity in this interesting
field of inquiry ; and as all correct notions of
Egyptian chronology must rest on a determina-

tion of the period at which that monarch assumed or exercised the supreme power . . . we fix this important epoch . . . by taking the mean of six estimates, viz. : 2256 B.C." But Abraham's date, he adds with assurance, is 2153 B.C.

The writer on Babylon says : " Passing over the early portion of Babylonian history which is obscure and doubtful, we shall limit ourselves to a short account of the subversion of the Kingdom in the time of Cyrus." He quotes with approval the statement of Herodotus : " The priests pretended that some of their books, in which their historical transactions and revolutions were all compared with the courses of the stars, were thousands of years old." The disbelief of Herodotus and the scepticism of the cyclopædist have been effectually answered by the discovery and the marvellous decipherment of the cuneiform records.

Philology. The inquiries into the origin of language were beset by similar restrictions. It was assumed that Hebrew must have been the first language, that all others must have traces of their common parent, and lists of similarity in vocabulary with the classical languages were provided. The article on Philology, discussing the origin of the letters, says : " The truth seems to be that letters were an antediluvian invention handed down by Noah to the Chaldæans and originating among the posterity of Cain." The writer on the " Alphabet " is less sanguine. He concludes that " the attempt made to illustrate the invention of writing by that of language proves invariably to be an impotent effort to explain one unknown thing by another. The invention of alphabetic writing is, in truth, an inexplicable mystery. We cannot touch it in any way or approach it on any side."

Such was the general conception of the beginning of history that was current a hundred years ago. In the interval there has been extensive observation and earnest study of heaven and earth. Evidence has been accumulated which has thrown an entirely new light upon the past.

Modern cosmogony from Astronomy. The stars of heaven used to be compared with the sand on the seashore as a symbol of infinity. The unaided human vision can perceive stars of the fifth or sixth magnitude, and the total of visible stars is set down at about seven thousand, of which the observer can only see one-half at a time. The telescope with the aid of photography discloses over a hundred million stars. The measurement of distance in time and space has become more precise, as well as vastly more comprehensive. If a penny piece be taken to represent the outer fringe of the solar system, the orbit of Neptune (3000 million miles from the Sun), and if the penny be placed about the middle of a ten-acre field, the boundary of the field would touch our nearest celestial neighbour among the stars. It takes four years for its light-rays to reach us, though they travel at the rate of 190,000 miles per second. The Sun and the Moon served as discordant chronometers for early interpreters of the planetary motions, but they have to be replaced by " light years " in the study of the stellar heavens. A modern cosmogony has to discover a cosmic symmetry which will include the Milky Way and all the furniture of space. The Sun and his planets, on one of which we live, has become insignificant in magnitude and splendour when compared with many of the constellations. The problems of the solar system have at the same time become more definitely isolated. The motions of the planets round the central Sun, their density and rotation, their satellites and rings, their conformity to the plane of the zodiac, the elements of which they are composed have been carefully observed and verified, and the almanacs satisfy the simple critic by their accurate prediction of eclipse. By comparison with observed changes in certain regions of the stellar heavens, credible theories are offered to account for certain phases in the past of the solar system. These transformations are held to require tens or even a hundred millions of years. Such results depend on the assumption that the laws of motion and force, which have been discovered in the last few centuries of human history, have been valid for all times and places; and that no other agency has ever intervened to modify the application of these laws. It is clear that a modern cosmogony has a more complicated task than the ancient philosophers had to face. The Biblical cosmography is built upon a superficial observation of heaven and earth; the eye and the imagination were more active than the reason in constructing the early picture of the World.

From Geology. When modern science turns its attention from our horizons to our home on earth, it discovers how comparatively brief has been man's presence on this planet. Mother Earth existed long ages before we came upon it. She passed through many stages in being prepared as a place for us. Continents were arranged and rearranged, oceans were duly distributed, mountains and plains were set in order. In course of time somehow life appeared on earth and flourished mightily in many forms. In those early days there were giant growths:

the ferns were as trees, and the mammoth was but little among beasts. Last of all, at the eleventh hour, as it were, man appeared to fight for dominion over the creatures. He is the youngest of the animals; brief life is here his portion. His days are as a handbreadth, and his age is as nothing compared with that of his inferiors.

When we ask Anatomy, What is man? the answer is, That our bodies, so wondrously made as they seem, are compounded of identically the same elements as the plants, the animals, and Mother Earth. In form and structure, man differs but little from the higher animals. Our brain indeed is larger, we have some advantage in the dome of the skull; the opposable thumb gives our hand a greater value; above all, we stand upright; nevertheless, bone for bone and muscle for muscle, we are closely conformed to the beasts that perish.

On what is Religion founded? Men have run to and fro, and knowledge has been increased; the modern framework for a picture of human religion must accordingly differ from that which served the eighteenth century. The creative process must not be limited to four thousand years, but must be measured by " light years." Life has taken many forms, and the immutability of types

is not to be assumed as it had been tradi-
tionally. Terrestrial life is long prior to human
life ; and the prehistoric ages of mankind are
to the brief historic period almost as a hundred
to one. When we find men recording the
chronicles of their transactions, we have to
realise that behind them lay the unrecorded
legacy of human experience from a quarter of a
million years. The events of unforgotten history
were conditioned by the bodily and spiritual
capacities acquired from this long prehistoric
human past. Before history began, languages
were formed. The mental processes, the dominant
ideas, the instinctive fidelity to logic of the various
races can be detected in the words they have
created. "There is nothing," said Leibnitz,
"that will furnish greater assistance in investigat-
ing the remote origins of peoples than the comparison of their languages." The vocabulary
of all languages is sufficient to show that religious
experience had been sufficiently real to induce
the prehistoric makers of language to invent
names for their feelings and for their deities.
The subconscious self, the embryo, the influences
of a long unrecorded past have their place in
estimating the forces which moulded religion.
But the intellectual curiosity, which impelled the
ancients to interpret themselves and the world,

is the same which has led to the achievements of modern science.

Religion inspires scientific inquiry but does not depend upon it. It may be said that Astronomy and Geology are not necessary to religion; that a man may be honest and God-fearing, although he knows nothing about the modern sciences. It is happily true that the measure of a man's knowledge is not a measure of his religion. But religion can never escape the duty of vindicating itself to reason, although reason has a very subordinate part in creating the religious temperament Hence the Bible begins by offering to intelligence a survey of the visible world and defining man's place in it. What has been placed first in the Bible, however, is one of the latest results of Hebrew reflection. Hebrew religion was not created out of nothing. The experience of a thousand years is mirrored in the Old Testament; and the raw material can be detected out of which prophets, priests, and poets moulded their spiritual experience. The Hebrew Bible is not arranged according to the order in which its several books were produced. From Creation to the year 562 B.C. is comprised in the section which now begins with Genesis and ends with 2 Kings. The Chronicler goes back again to Adam and gives a duplicate version of the same period, omitting what does not interest him, and magnifying the place in history of the institutions and ceremonial in which he is supremely concerned. The five Mosaic books are composed of codes of law, which have been revised and re-edited more than once; and the pervasive scheme of the Pentateuch comes from the age of Ezra and Nehemiah, about 450 B.C. Careful study of the Bible has succeeded in connecting the several documents with the age in which they originated, and is thus enabled to perceive how the life and the literature were connected. Hebrew religion had discovered its greatest verities long before it began to speculate on pre-human and prehistoric conditions; and the message of the prophets does not depend on any particular theory of the remote past. The rise and growth of Israel's beliefs can be best understood by following the course of events in time, rather than by carrying back the reflections of the later wisdom into primordial origins.

Israel's history from 1000 B.C. to 600 B.C. The period of the Monarchy offers the best evidence for discovering the earlier phases of Hebrew religion. The appointment of kings meant the beginning of a life that was national, in succession to a series of tribal episodes. What Wallace and Bruce did for Scotland, Saul and David did for Israel.

After their time a class of official recorders came
into existence. The detachment from personal
interests, imposed upon these secretaries by their
office, is an incentive to the composition of
history. The authors of the books of Samuel
and Kings appear to have used contemporary
evidence in their description of the main events.
The section which relates the Court life of David
in Jerusalem and the competition for the throne
at the accession of Solomon, may have been
written by an eye-witness. This historical restraint does not pervade all the sources used by
the final editor. Popular interest loved to tell
how the shepherd lad overcame the giant in his
armour, but was indifferent to the long lists of
officials. The stories of Elisha satisfied a fond-
ness for marvel which the Court annalist did not
care to indulge. The moral criteria for pro-
nouncing a verdict on the reigns of the several
kings, presuppose the standard prescribed by
Deuteronomy. But the compilers and editors
have supplied their own framework without
obliterating the living influences of the period.
For the second half of the monarchy, there is a
source of information of unquestioned value.
The authentic parts of the written discourses
of the Prophets bring us face to face with the
ideas and activities of their time and place.

The chronology is also sufficiently certified. A total eclipse recorded in the Assyrian annals gives a fixed point in the year 763 B.C. ; and the Assyrian references to various kings from Ahab to Manasseh supply an approximate corroboration from Astronomy and profane history to the succession of kings in the Bible. David's reign of forty years began about 1017 B.C. ; the Temple was built 973 B.C. and was destroyed by the Chaldæans in 586 B.C. The Northern Kingdom, formed by the succession of the Ten Tribes under Jeroboam, began in 937 B.C., and came to an end with the fall of its capital, Samaria, in 722 B.C. The Northern seceders, though more influential among their neighbours, have a smaller place in the history. They had kept records, and had their own traditions of the Patriarchs, which were later included in the Pentateuch, and they had the prophets Elijah and Hosea. The second edition of Hebrew history in the Chronicles practically ignores the Northern Kingdom. Their contribution to Hebrew religion was of minor importance ; and it is to the community that was centred in Jerusalem that the development of religion was ultimately due.

It is during the period of the Monarchy (1017–586 B.C.) that the distinctive character of Hebrew religion was made clear. The rest of the world kept going on in its traditional way—only in Greece was there any sign of fresh vitality and mental achievement.   The war at Troy had found a poet who was to make his heroes sure of admiration for all time. The *Iliad*, too, has a religion, and became a Bible for Alexander the Great; but Homer would make no modern converts to his faith, and after the Greek philosophers he became insufficient even for his own compatriots.   Egypt, despite her artistic skill and her magnificent monuments, was patiently carrying the burden of absurdity in the care of her soul, prostrating herself before hawks and crocodiles, constructing costly mausoleums for her sacred bulls.   Assyria, though powerful in arms, was feeble and foolish in religion and brutally wanting in humanity.   It is among the Hebrews alone that something new and true reveals itself during these five centuries.

New thoughts in Israel.

Measured by skill in creating material civilisation, the Hebrews were inferior to many of their contemporaries.   They could not sharpen their plough-irons when the Philistines took the smiths away.   They were but poor pupils of their foreign teachers in moulding earthenware for domestic purposes. They had to rely on Hiram, king of Tyre, for skilled artisans to make their Temple beautiful.

Hebrews unskilled in arts and crafts.

When international trade became possible, the imports which impressed them most were apes and peacocks. When they decided to cut a channel for bringing the waters of the Virgin's Fountain within the Walls of Jerusalem, they began at both ends of the intervening rock but missed each other, at the first attempt, in the interior of the hill. Some workman was so impressed with this underground adventure, that he scratched on the roof of the tunnel the story of their success, in what is now known as the Siloam inscription. In agriculture their success was only moderate. They had been nomads long ago and were never reconciled to the drudgery of crofters. Compared with Sinai, Canaan could be described as " a land flowing with milk and honey "; but the Central Highlands require as much vigilance and industry to yield a living as Caledonia. Under the kings the population was probably never so numerous or so well fed as under the Romans. In war they had during these five centuries constant struggles to maintain their independence, which they lost in the end. In military power they were insignificant when compared with the great powers around them— Egypt, Babylonia, the Hittites, the Philistines from Crete. Deuteronomy approves universal military service, with many considerate exemptions, but dislikes horses, chariots, and war. They had no enthusiasm for the sea or for ships. The home of rest in Jerusalem was to have plenty of water but no ships. Our version under King James was made before the Armada was forgotten ; and Britannia gives a music to her rendering which is not in the original Hebrew. " But there the glorious LORD will be unto us a place of broad rivers and streams ; wherein shall go no galley with oars, neither shall gallant ship pass thereby " (Isa. 33[21]). In general capacity the Hebrews were similar to their smaller neighbours, Edom, Moab, Ammon, Midian, just as they were allied in blood and language, and customs, with these tribes. The world in general had meanwhile a confused inheritance of primitive religious beliefs and scruples—polytheism, animism, fetishism, magic, astrology, divination, and such-like. How did the Hebrews contrive to lay aside their share in this inheritance, and to discover true principles concerning the being of God and the soul of man ?

Religion under Samuel. The life of Samuel is so written as to show the religious temper of his time. They have a definite Name, JHVH, for the Deity. It is a personal name ; and in giving a name to his two boys, Samuel reverently includes the sacred name in their designations " Joel " and " Abijah." The Philistines have naturally a god of their own, Dagon, who is served by priests and diviners and is provided with a house. An oath has great sanctity, great enough to make Saul ready to slay Jonathan on the very day he and his servant had discomfited the Philistines. The commonest oaths are " as JHVH lives " and " as thy soul liveth." Ultimate reality for them is the soul of man and the spirit of God—both alive. God is mysterious in power and purpose, and some men are better able than others to understand divine things. There are priests who pass on their knowledge from father to son, and these families are entrusted with the care of the sanctuaries and the offering of sacrifices at the annual festivals. But the Divine Spirit cannot be compelled to remain with a hereditary aristocracy ; a sure house depends on faithful priests. The Spirit selects the souls that are most responsive to the Divine purpose—Saul to be a king; and when Saul has received the Spirit he makes up his standing army from " a band of men whose hearts God had touched." Others are chosen to be prophets, soldiers, humble agents in a scheme of which they have no knowledge.

2

Men are perfectly well aware when the Spirit is with them, and when it has forsaken them. Saul, who has many noble elements in his character, becomes melancholy and ineffectual as soon as he feels himself forsaken. Music can soothe him ; but when no answer comes, " neither by dreams, nor by Urim, nor by prophets " (1 Sam. 28⁶), his despair sends him to a medium who is in touch with a " control " and can exercise necromancy. A child like Samuel, born in answer to prayer, and dedicated from infancy to the service of the sanctuary, is likely to receive the Spirit, though the gift was rare at the time. The aged Eli has long ago lost the faculty ; his sons, if they had any feeling for the Spirit, could not be covetous and immoral as they were in their sacred office. Hence Eli accepts without hesitation as the word of God the first utterance of the child prophet, who has to announce the doom of Eli and his house.

In many details the working of the Spirit is described in ways that have been fully confirmed by the experience of later ages. JHVH hears and may answer sincere prayer, and guides the soul that is obedient. He continues His purposes through succeeding generations, chastises insolence and cruelty, and fulfils the just desire. The Master of the Universe, as moderns know it, would not be misconceived by imputing such attributes to His nature.

Magic. On the other hand, there is much in that age which was superseded by the prophets. The Ark of wood, which was the symbol of a covenant between JHVH and His people, was invested with magical powers. Sleeping near it, the child Samuel hears divine voices. After losing one battle, the Army sends for the Ark, expecting to be invincible in their counter-attack. But a flaw in procedure is followed by heavier defeat. When the Ark is captured, Eli's heart is broken because the glory had departed from Israel. Among its captors, the presence of the Ark causes Dagon to fall into fragments, and brings plague-boils on the inhabitants of Ashdod, Gath, and Ekron. To get rid of it, two milch cows are yoked to a wagon bearing the Ark, and against natural inclination, "lowing as they went," the cows take the road to Beth-shemesh. The Hebrews of Beth-shemesh, with irreverent curiosity, look into the Ark, and 70,000 of them perish in consequence. "Who is able to stand before JHVH, this holy God?" (1 Sam. 6[20]). "If a man sin against JHVH, who shall intreat for him?" (2[25]). The motive of the stories is to imply that there are dangers in life, and that well - meaning ignorance may have fatal results.

An apology for magic. Belief in magic is sometimes considered to be the lowest phase of primitive religion ; and it still makes life for many uncultivated races a needless struggle against imaginary evils. The postulate of magic is that mysterious powers beset the life of man, but that if man only knew the proper spell, these powers, divine and diabolic, would be forced to obey his will. If an ancient magician could be shown the working of the telegraph, he could assert that he had always maintained that this effect could be secured with the proper spell. The magician would not be surprised that contact with a wire conveying a strong current of electricity should cause the death of a good man or a bad man impartially. The error of the magician lay in his ascribing such effects to the direct volition of a personal God.

The Seer. Various incidents are related to show the reverence due to the man of God. He has powers which ordinary people do not possess. He might tell where the lost asses were to be found ; but decent neighbours would not like to ask his help unless they could give a small present in return. He has prevision of details, and uses this vision to convince his agents of the divine authority of his instructions. He can also command the thunder and bring rain in wheat harvest. He anoints kings ; before any great enterprise, he seeks to ascertain the will of God. He requires strict obedience ; and even justifiable disobedience — as when Saul himself offered sacrifice because Samuel was late, or when he spared Agag—involves the heaviest penalties. Such stories appealed to the common temperament of the time ; and, although there were conscious impostors among the companies of the prophets, the case of Samuel himself shows that he was not misled by current superstitions into serious error in the supreme purposes of his life.

Inspiration in prophets. When we turn from the lifetime of Samuel and select the dominant influences of the next four centuries, it is clear that the prophets are the creators of Israel's religion. They are not only the source of fervent feeling, but they exhibit a growing intelligence which is applied to every region of human experience. They pronounce judgment on social customs and enterprises, and act as a conscience for kings. They make King David conscious of his crimes, convict him of injustice, and kindle in him penitence and the desire to make all possible amends. They keep alive the consciousness that

JHVH is not like the gods of other peoples, but requires the exclusive loyalty of the nation. The figure of Elijah has been somewhat transfigured by a later hero-worship, but his tenacity had some right to be magnified. In his days there was a danger that the Hebrews, who had conformed to the agriculture of the Canaanites, should also adopt their worship of the Baals at the local sanctuaries. King Ahab had married Jezebel, a princess from Tyre, and had allowed his queen to introduce Tyrian priests and customs. Elijah knew that the Spirit he served was not like the local Baals or Dagon of Ashdod. JHVH had been with their fathers long before they had had a local home in Palestine. Hence when his hopes were low, Elijah is found at Horeb, the mount of God ; and here his faith is renewed, and he is taught that neither through the storm, nor the earthquake, nor the lightning, but through " the still small voice " is the guidance of God to be found. His pure theism inspires him with a clear perception of what is right in human conduct. To get possession of Naboth's vineyard, King Ahab consented to Jezebel's advice to contrive the death of the unwilling owner. In daring to be a critic and avenger of the royal crime, Elijah makes himself a memorable figure in Oriental life.

Oral tradition collected and written. Elijah and the earlier prophets do not seem to have committed their discourses to writing; but by the time of Elijah the stories of ancient Hebrew history had probably been collected and written. In their written form, these stories of their ancestors retain rare literary merit, and have proved a model of style to many ages. This quality arises from the fact that they were interesting, often told, and familiar to everybody. They were not meant to edify but to entertain, to brighten leisure, to create good fellowship when people met together. For the children, education meant that they should know all these stories and be able to tell them well and faithfully. To be ignorant about Abraham or Joseph or Moses, to be unable to tell why Bethel or Hebron or Shechem was famous, would be to be uneducated like the Philistines.

The Ephraim stories (E) and the Judah stories (J). Two collections of early oral tradition are intertwined with the narrative of our Pentateuch. One of these is traced to Ephraim, and is often referred to among students by the symbol E. The other probably took form in Judah, and is styled J. These two documents have such a similarity as is found between the Gospels of St. Mark and St. Matthew. They both trace the experiences of Abraham in Canaan, the visit of Jacob to Egypt, the career of Joseph, the Exodus and the giving of the Ten Words in Sinai, the march through the desert, the conquests east of Jordan, and the battles west of the Jordan. The recorders of the traditions have arranged them so as to exhibit the rise and progress of the nation prior to the monarchy.

How do E and J begin their books ? The Ephraim stories do not venture to look back so far as the Flood, but begin with Abraham. They are responsible for the chapter which condemns human sacrifice by describing how Abraham was prevented from offering his son Isaac. The story of Joseph is told with much artistic skill so as to show how Divine Providence can turn even the sins of men to a source of final blessing. "As for you," says Joseph to his brethren who had sold him into slavery, "ye meant evil against me; but God meant it for good, to bring to pass, as it is this day, to save much people alive" (Gen. 50^{20}). When good men are dying they may see the future more clearly; and Jacob's last words in Egypt are a promise that his descendants would not remain in Egypt. "God shall be with you, and bring you again unto the land of your fathers."

"Genesis" according to J. The Judæan parallel stories have the same outline of characters and events, but make Judah prominent among the twelve sons of Jacob, and are most interested in

Hebron and neighbourhood. They supply a preface dealing with primeval history. They include an account of the Deluge, a relic of mythology in the notice of the giants, an explanation of how things began, the domestication of the animals, the discovery of wine, of music, of working with metals, of city building, of the formation of different races and languages. Reflection and study have been required to supply this preface to history. The quest for origins leads the compiler to seek for an absolute beginning. His main interest is not in the stars but on earth—a dry land depending on rain and irrigation. The Maker of man is JHVH, who moulded the moistened earth into human form and by the Divine inspiration man became a living soul. Then the garden of Eden was made, and plants and animals, and finally Eve to be of kindred nature with Adam. The preface to the Judæan stories supplies a psychology which has had profound influence on subsequent thought, but this point will receive consideration at a later stage.

When did men learn the true Divine Name? The stories collected in Ephraim and Judah were not primarily meant to evoke religious feeling, but to satisfy curiosity and to foster patriotism. But both compilers are keenly interested in purely religious questions. How does man know the name of God ? The Ephraim collection tells how the ineffable Name was first revealed to Moses in Midian. To seek any derivation of this word would be impious ; it was enough for Moses to say to his kinsmen in Egypt, " I AM hath sent me unto you " (Ex. 3^{14}). Consistently with this account, the Ephraim stories always call the Divine Being by the name Elohim in pre-Mosaic times. On the other hand, the Judæan stories assume that the name JHVH was known from time immemorial. As far back as the days of Enos, son of Seth, son of Adam, he says : " Then began men to call upon the name of JHVH " (Gen. 4^{26}). The post-exilic contributor to the Pentateuch has also a definite theory on the revelation of the sacred name (Ex. 6^3).

No Hebrew mythology. Compared with the history of religion in general, is there anything distinctive in these earliest Hebrew Scriptures ? Every race with any imagination has a mythology telling about the birth of gods and goddesses, their combats and counsels, their fantastic doings, good or bad. The Hebrews may have shared a Semitic mythology like the Babylonian ; the late books produced in the names of Enoch, Abraham, and others just before the Christian era may use suppressed traditions ; our poet, Milton, may be well guided in his re-creation of primeval Hebrew phantasy. But these earliest parts of the Hebrew Bible have left polytheism far behind. Their God is One : there are no varied divine characters to figure in an Olympian drama. The word " Elohim " is plural in form, but is deliberately meant to be a plural of majesty ; it requires in grammar to have its verb or adjective in the singular number. There is no separate word for " goddess " in the Hebrew language. By the time of the kings the instinct and imagination of the Hebrews conceived JHVH as one ; and their peculiar knowledge was traced back to Moses, who had led them from bondage to freedom. One other treasure had been gained— the Ten Commandments in their shortest form. In these ten short sentences the humblest Hebrew had commandments sufficient to show him his duty to his neighbour, his parents, and his God.

The revelation of ethical monotheism. It is hard to find any nation producing within half a century four great personalities like Amos and Hosea, Isaiah of Jerusalem and Micah. These four prophets flourished between 760 and 700 B.C., and their gravest anticipations were fulfilled by the destruction of the Northern Kingdom in 722 B.C. These men faced and conquered the terrors that haunted human life, the morbid fancies of men's hearts, the demons and spirits, the crowd of false gods. They raised human nature to a higher level ; it is to them that we owe the axioms of sound religion.

The message they receive is the same in substance though it has come through four independent messengers. It is that God is One and God is righteous ; and the four messages can therefore be ascribed to the same Person. What led these men to reject the common belief in many gods ? Bees have their queen, and stags their leader ; men have their monarchs, should not spirits also have a supreme spirit ? The earth is the centre of all we see : the parts are many, yet together they must form a whole—a whole which includes all the parts and yet is something different from their sum. They had their own home, and like all their neighbours they had their own Deity. Long ago their fathers had spoken of Him as El Shaddai, and also as Elohim ; but since Moses had been told the real name, they had abandoned anonymous Divinity and had recognised only JHVH as true God. Such considerations may have appealed to idle reflection, which was satisfied with a probable God for ontological or teleological reasons. But these plausible analogies and other arguments, though they may assist reason in vindicating religious experience, are negligible to the prophets. The soul of man is the innermost sanctuary of human experience, as Elijah had been taught. Personality is the highest attainment of the cosmic process. All languages strive to invent adequate words for the Self, the soul of a human being conscious of its own unity. It is to the soul of the prophets that the Unity of God is first revealed. They can tell how the Spirit first came to them— to Amos while he was a humble shepherd, to Isaiah during a service in the Temple, to Hosea amid domestic tragedy, to Jeremiah before he was born, just as it came to Mohammed, the prophet of Arabia, in the time of ignorant idolatry. It is to such prophets in contact with the Spirit of God that the unity of God becomes the deepest certainty of human knowledge.

Amos. Amos acquires his experience, not through men, but in the solitude of the hills overlooking the Dead Sea. He is not, as Jerome said, rustic in his style any more than Robert Burns was rustic. His poems appear to have been made by reciting aloud his perceptions as they came to him in the country. He appears at the Royal sanctuary in Bethel, his awe for JHVH overcoming his shyness before priests and crowds. His announcement is that JHVH is righteous, and means to establish righteousness on earth. Israel, despite her prosperity and joyous festivals, is blind, thinking that God is her Defender and Patron, whose function is to make Palestine a safe place for Israel. But Israel is unrighteous, careless about the clean decencies of human life, insulting the sanctity of kindly brotherhood, taking bribes to reject the pleas of the innocent, making religion contemptible by a ritual which dishonours God. Because God is just, He has punished Moab, the Philistines, Edom, and Tyre. If God be righteous, as Amos knew He was, could He become the Protector of wilful unrighteousness? Therefore unrighteous Israel must expect destruction in " the day of the Lord," which day was now imminent. Though stars and seas and mountains have to be demolished, and all the nations have to perish by their own folly, the righteous purpose of God must be fulfilled.

Hosea.   Hosea's warning to Bethel is not less stern; but punishment of crime is not the consummation of Divine governance. The prophet himself had succeeded in kindling penitence in an unfaithful woman, and by pure love had restored her soul to health. The same redemptive pity in God will follow erring Israel and enable her ultimately to walk in the true way. Right and justice are blended with pity and grace. As the modern Jew prepares himself for Divine Service by winding a ribbon thrice round the middle finger, he recites the words of Hos. 2[19, 20] : " And I will betroth thee unto me for ever : yea, I will betroth thee unto me in righteousness, and in judgment, and in loving-kindness, and in mercy : I will even betroth thee unto me in faithfulness : and thou shalt know the Lord." The loyal regard of a good wife for a good husband is the kind of love that is required as the sovereign duty of man to God in the highest form of Christian faith. The spirit of Hosea has had more influence in Scotland than most of the other prophets, because John Morison, minister of Canisbay in Caithness in 1780, con-veyed the divine encouragement to us in the 30th Paraphrase :

> " Come let us to the Lord our God
> With contrite hearts return."

Through this Scottish version Hosea speaks to Scotland, appealing without offence to strength and tenderness, to courage and compassion.

Isaiah of Jerusalem. In Isaiah of Jerusalem (740–701 B.C.) prophecy invites and deserves universal attention. " Hear, O heavens, and give ear, O earth : for JHVH hath spoken " (Isa. 1[2]). Isaiah is a master of noble thoughts and majestic language. He has seen the Divine King in His glory; and the petty arrogance of man at his mightiest is altogether vanity. Like Amos and Hosea, he sees that judgment is at hand; but he endeavours to direct the policy of the State so that Judah need not share the fate of Samaria. He teaches that a purified remnant, a holy seed, will survive the national disaster; that this better community will be established in an inviolable Zion, under a Messianic King with perfect attributes. The ideal King of Zion shall be the Judge of nations, and shall teach them to abolish war for ever. " They shall not hurt nor destroy in all my holy mountain: for the earth shall be full of the knowledge of JHVH, as the waters cover the sea." The Spirit of JHVH is called the spirit of wisdom and understanding, the spirit of knowledge and of the fear of the Lord.

Isaiah's ideal future includes a local element in postulating the inviolability of Zion. In the year 701 B.C. Sennacherib and the Assyrians devastated Judah, plundering forty-six cities and taking 200,150 prisoners, who were deported as captives. It seemed certain that Jerusalem could not escape; but by some means it did.

" And the might of the Gentile, unsmote by the sword,
    Hath melted like snow in the glance of the Lord."

This deliverance vindicated the dogma of Isaiah. But Micah, the contemporary of Isaiah, said:

" Zion shall be plowed as a field, and Jerusalem shall become heaps, and the mountain of the Temple as the high places of the forest " (Mic. 3^{12}). A century later Jeremiah had sore difficulties in trying to remove the false confidence inspired among his contemporaries by this detail in the discourses of Isaiah.

Judah, 700–600 B.C. The century that followed these four great prophets began with an ineffectual attempt of Hezekiah to abolish some objectionable popular practices. A strong opposition arose under King Manasseh, and for fifty years prophecy was silent. The disciples of the prophets were persecuted, but they remained loyal to the new spirit and made a fresh study of the past history of their people. The result appeared in a revised version of the Mosaic Law, to be found in our Deuteronomy. Under Josiah, the new king, who had been reared under prophetic influence, this code of law was adopted as the national constitution in 622 B.C. King and people assented to this solemn league and covenant, and a reformation followed. Local sanctuaries were replaced by the Temple in Jerusalem ; sacred pillars and idolatrous emblems were destroyed, and the ideals of the prophets became part of the central system of religion.

In the generation before the fall of Jerusalem

there were several prophets of minor importance. The Scythians overran Asia for some years ; and the effects of their raids are described by Zephaniah in words which inspired the famous hymn " Dies Iræ," the Day of Wrath.   Nahum and Habakkuk are concerned with the end of Nineveh and of Assyrian power and cruelty.   The greatest figure of the period is Jeremiah of Anathoth.

Jeremiah, 626-586 B.C.   It was Jeremiah's fate to watch the decline and fall of Judah.   Assyria was conquered by the Medes and Chaldæans, who then fought with Egypt for world-power.   Placed between such combatants, Judah could not tell which power to conciliate.   Jeremiah consistently recommended neutrality, and for advising surrender to the Chaldæans he suffered imprisonment.   In 597 the Chaldæans deported 10,000 of the leading citizens and imposed a tribute on Judah.   The last king intrigued with Egypt, provoked another siege, and was deported with his people after the sack of Jerusalem.   The acrostic poems lamenting the disaster to the. Holy City are ascribed to Jeremiah, and they are not inappropriate to the dominant mood of his life.

The discovery of the individual is often claimed as the supreme merit of this prophet.   He certainly tells us more of himself than the other prophets, and he is a strong advocate of self-

determination. He resents the coercion which
called him into life in an age when the world
was out of joint. He rebels against inheriting
the penalties which had to follow the sins of
Manasseh. He hopes no children may be born
or reared in such a time of trouble ; and, almost
singular in Hebrew history, he elects for himself
a celibate life. He has a genuine love for his
own race, and begins to be an intercessor with
God as well as a preacher of the Divine Word.
His ethical standard remains high and his theism
pure. " Will ye steal, murder, and commit
adultery, and swear falsely, and burn incense
unto Baal ? " (Jer. 7⁹). " Hearken ye not to your
prophets, nor to your diviners, nor to your dreams,
nor to your sorcerers, which speak unto you, saying,
Ye shall not serve the king of Babylon " (Jer. 27⁹).

But the submission of a nature so susceptible,
so self-conscious, and so headstrong is all the
more impressive. He resigns himself to the
antenatal call to prophesy and finds a way for
his soul to reach health and peace, whatever
outward events may happen. His self-determination issues in accepting suffering without
bitterness ; and he sets himself to prepare some
compatriots for the loss of land and king, temple
and law-books. He discovered that it would be
hopeless to induce any nation to choose such a

fate, but he might succeed in kindling a new life in individuals and writing the law on their heart. Then they, too, would be prophets, led by the Spirit, proof against any foreign domination or discouragement.

The Chaldæan Ghetto. A final test had yet to be applied to the religion of the prophets. Was their belief in One Righteous God a genuine discovery or a comfortable hypothesis ? Could other souls feel the Divine power sufficiently to make them do right in spite of obstacles ? The probation took place when the Jerusalem refugees were compelled to spend fifty years in a Chaldæan Ghetto. Would they, like the Ten Tribes, adopt the habits of their conquerors and disappear ? They were a smaller fragment in a greater mass, and their survival less likely on that account. But the thoughts of the prophets had been longer in circulation ; and once apprehended, these thoughts were not easily discarded. Deuteronomy had given a watchword and challenge to the simplest Hebrew in the formula: " JHVH our God, JHVH is ONE " (Deut. 6⁴). Moreover, the exiles in Chaldæa were sustained by the great prophets Ezekiel and the Second Isaiah.

Isaiah of the Exile. The national fortunes were most miserable. Conquered in war, torn from their native land, their sanctuaries dishonoured, their labour prescribed by force, their children growing up to be slaves, how could they escape despair and pessimism? Yet it was in these conditions that the Second Isaiah proclaimed a radiant optimism, and declared their destiny to be supremely glorious. He is convinced that verified knowledge can never yield homage to transparent absurdity; and he teaches his fellow-exiles to give a rational defence of their faith. Never again do Hebrews show serious signs of adopting polytheism. Further, Isaiah knows that his pure religion is the sovereign good required by all men. The highest service one nation can do for another is to inspire it with true religion. This service the handful of despised refugees had the power to do for all nations. Isaiah dispels the selfish and vainglorious patriotism of preceding centuries, and aspires to a distinction which is universal and spiritual. The promises to their fathers long ago, that their seed should be for a blessing to all races, were to be fulfilled by making their conquerors partners in the knowledge of God and of duty, which had been revealed to them.

The reward of God's Servant. They had good news, and it would be their glory to diffuse the light among all nations. What reward might they expect from heaven and earth? Rectitude,

according to Deuteronomy, would be followed
by length of happy days in Judæa ; yet within a
single generation Judæa had been lost. Jeremiah
had lived a good life, yet he was rewarded with
imprisonment, exile, and perhaps martyrdom.
If obeying the voice of God involved these rewards,
would it not be better to disobey ? Could the
penalty of disobedience be any more severe than
the lifelong torture of Jeremiah ? Nay, said the
Second Isaiah, the Servant of God will discount
suffering in advance. He will not measure the
reward very carefully ; but he will not fail nor
be discouraged till he have established right on
earth. Whether there be any immortality or
not, God has called us to proclaim His will among
men ; and the Servant of God must obey the
Divine command at all costs.

The birth of true religion. Here then we arrive at something new
among the nations of antiquity. Two
or three races began early to write about
their fathers ; all the rest passed away indifferent
and inarticulate. Egypt and Babylon could
build cities and even irrigate rivers, but their
thoughts about God and man are surprisingly
crude and irrational. In the wilderness, between
these two great civilisations, a few tribes of
Semitic nomads contrive to establish a precarious
hold in the Highlands west and east of Jordan.

They are fused into one nation for a century, but fall apart. The larger half disappears from history after two hundred and fifty years. The smaller fragment survives for one hundred and thirty years longer, and is subjected to the same temporal disasters. Judah walks loose in the fiery furnace, and emerges from her trials with a new vitality.

The exceptional result is ascribed by their spirits to an exceptional cause. The Living God, to whom they had yielded their souls, had given them the light of life and had led them through all their trials and hardships. Their thoughts of God and man, their interpretation of five hundred years of their own history, have formed a text-book of religion for mankind.

LECTURE II.

HEBREW RELIGION FROM CYRUS TO VESPASIAN—530 B.C.–70 A.D.

Axioms of religion. IT appeared from our survey of the five hundred years under the monarchy that the Hebrew prophets had discovered the first principles of true religion. They affirmed that God is One, Incomparable, Unique in such a sense that there can be no second, any more than there can be a second universe. They also called men to a new conception of duty, because they had perceived the holiness of God. The survivors of the nation in exile had so apprehended the truth of these principles, that they accepted adverse physical conditions rather than relinquish their convictions. The present Lecture will trace the fortune and the influence of these ideas through another period of six hundred years—from the time when Cyrus the Persian gave the Hebrews a new lease of life in Judah and Jerusalem, till the year when the Romans under Vespasian and Titus again reduced the

Temple to ashes and scattered the Jews among the Gentiles.

Survival of knowledge.   It should not be assumed in advance that great discoveries in knowledge are certain to survive in future generations. Each brood of children begins from ignorance ; and only through active effort, aided by careful teaching, can they preserve the intellectual gains of their seniors. Classical learning was ignored for centuries in Europe ; its vitality had not perished and its rediscovery was followed by a revival of intelligence. Even among the Greeks, who appreciated the dramas of their greatest poets, very few of these masterpieces have survived ; some of those we have remain through the accident that they were used as school books. Electricity has always existed, though men knew nothing about it except the fear they felt at thunder and lightning. Without continuous experience and training, the current knowledge of electricity might vanish like the knowledge of the Greek " Fire " which saved Constantinople from the ships of the Arabs. The mere fact that prophetic religion survived at all through the next six hundred years implies that succeeding generations were, one after another, independently convinced of its truth. It also follows that the God who spoke through the prophets is, as they said, the Living God—caring for the fathers and for their children's children unto all generations.

Survival of nations. Ideas may vanish, records may become undecipherable, and even races may disappear. The survival of the Hebrews of the Second Jerusalem is more significant when contrasted with the story of the Ten Tribes, who called the capital they had built for themselves the " Watch Tower," or Samaria. The name they chose for their metropolis on the " egg-shaped " hill, expressed their fixed determination to be vigilant against the approach of every danger. Yet their State existed only two and a half centuries from beginning to end. The Assyrians deported the population, but introduced settlers from Cutha and other Assyrian districts. The new colonists were troubled by lions, and sent for one of the Hebrew priests, who knew " the manner of the God of the land." They continued to serve their own gods and to include the local Hebrew deity, as they conceived Him, in their pantheon. Some of the original Hebrews still remained on the land, and they gradually merged themselves by intermarriage with the settlers. When Jerusalem was restored, this composite community offered to unite with the returned exiles ; but they were told they had no portion or rights in the Holy City. They agreed to have no dealings with Jerusalem, and established their own sanctuary on Mount Gerizim, henceforth holding the Southern Hebrews to be schismatics. They acknowledged as Holy Scriptures no more than the five books of the Mosaic Law, denying Divine authority to prophets, Psalms, and all the later Rabbinic traditions. They were, therefore, unlike the Jerusalem priest and Levite of apostolic days, freer to render first aid to a wounded stranger at the roadside. They thus acquire fame through the Gospel parable of the Good Samaritan. They never became powerful or numerous, though in the time of Justinian (c. 550 A.D.) the word " Samaritan " became a designation for " bank-clerks " in Constantinople ; and an insurrection at Nablus had to be sharply punished by the same emperor. The community is now reported to number one hundred and fifty-seven souls in all. They are the only distinct representatives of ancient Israel who have maintained an unbroken tenure of their land. Their High Priest is Isaac, son of Amram ; they still offer their sacrifices on Mount Gerizim, sprinkling the blood of the paschal lamb on the faces of the children. Their existence is a matter of rare interest ; and their renewed vitality would be welcomed by all who have felt the grace of the Good Samaritan.

The lost Ten Tribes. The loss of home and country meant the end of the Northern Israelites who had their capital in Samaria. Though they had been more important than Judah, they did not preserve the slender share in history which fell to the Samaritan remnant. The disappearance of the Ten Tribes has given rise to various reflections. They, too, were the children of Jacob, heirs to the promises ; they, too, shared the duty of becoming a blessing to all races. How did they forfeit their share in this great destiny ? In deference to such premises it is sometimes proposed to identify the descendants of the Northern Hebrews with living races who have taken new names, *e.g.* the Afghans, the Falashas of Abyssinia, or even the inhabitants of Great Britain. Oliver Cromwell was much impressed by the rumour that some of the lost Ten Tribes had been found in South America ; and his respect for Providence in history was not without influence in making him sanction the admission of Jews to England after they had been banished for centuries.

Feeble monotheism. The fate of the Ten Tribes yields this inference. Their belief in God had not yet become so vitally true to them as to make them steer their own course in spite of Assyrian control. The visions of Elijah and

Hosea were never shared by many, were never made common feeling by a law like Deuteronomy, were never made the fount of loyal devotion by the use of Psalms. No prophet like Ezekiel or the Second Isaiah inspired and sustained the faith of the exiles of Samaria in Assyria. Their theism was still semi - conscious, imperfectly assimilated, dependent on local customs and territorial accidents. At home they had used the sacred bull as an emblem of the Divinity; they would find better specimens of carving in the Assyrian cities. Probably they had harsher conditions of servitude than those imposed by the more humane Chaldæans on the captives of Judah. While grateful for Hosea and the Ephraim stories, history has to bid farewell to the Ten Tribes who seceded under Jeroboam, the son of Nebat, " who did sin, and who made Israel to sin."

Returned exiles. Henceforward it is with a fragment of the Hebrew nation that we have to deal. A remnant will return, a " holy seed " will be saved, Isaiah had said. When Cyrus became supreme in the Euphrates valley he authorised the return of the captive Jews from Chaldæa to Jerusalem. Under Solomon, Hebrews are estimated to have numbered about three million souls; by the end of the Exile they were reduced to about a hundred thousand. They had been fifty years away from home, and the few who had seen Jerusalem must have been over sixty years of age. Prisoners of war are glad enough to come home, and it is no proof of exceptional patriotism that about fifty thousand found their way back to Judah. But the great majority remained in Chaldæa, and prospered abundantly in commerce and learning. Unlike the Assyrian captives they never forget their religion, and were able to send substantial help to the new community in Jerusalem. The significant element in this period of their history is that the restoration was an answer to prayer. " Utter it even to the ends of the earth : JHVH hath redeemed his people." The faith of the exilic prophet had been marvellously confirmed by the course of events ; and without his inspiration the desire to return would have died away among the captives.

National penitence. What was this peculiar feeling which kept its owners alive while other races were disappearing ? By its own account, Hebrew religion had made the character of the patriarchs worthy of affectionate remembrance, and had moved their descendants to choose the hunger and freedom of the wilderness in preference to the task-work and flesh-pots of Egypt. The same Divine Spirit had kindled penitence in the people when they grew careless, and had assisted their deliverers in times of trial. It was for their sins that national freedom had been taken away from them. When Athens felt her power being broken, when her enemies were victorious on all fronts, when her empire was falling into fragments, she tried to comfort herself in the theatres with the comedies of Aristophanes. When Israel was in the same position, she said : " Let us search and try our ways, and turn again to the Lord " (Lam. 3[40]).

" He jests at scars who never felt a wound."

The probation of these two generations in a Chaldæan Ghetto had added unforgettable experience to the Hebrew record, and had repeated the distant deliverance from Egypt before their eyes. For the next six centuries Hebrew religion was cultivated in a little city-state, self-contained in the main but assisted by kinsmen loyal to the faith in foreign lands. Spiritual progress did not consist in the appearance of great prophetic personalities like Amos and Isaiah with fresh inspiration. But there was something more than the mere repetition of the phrases of the prophets in the recital of a statutory creed. Deuteronomy practically effected this, and thereby made the

prophetic formulæ maxims for the whole community.   There was something more than collect-
ing and recording the discourses of the great
prophets who had left no successors.   There was
an effort to make the man, who repeated the
words of Isaiah, " Holy, holy, holy," have some
distant approach to the feeling which Isaiah had
when he first used the words.   This effort led
to the prophetic interpretation of Hebrew history,
and inspired the search for unity in primeval
origins.   The final result was to enshrine the
prophetic spirit in a rigid code of Mosaic law
which dominated every detail of conduct and
discouraged independent thoughts.

Recon-   The picture of the New Jerusalem,
struction. as the Zionists from Chaldæa found
it, is preserved in the fragments of the addresses
of Haggai and Zechariah.   They were only about
fifty thousand who forsook the prospects of
Babylon ; but their hopes were high.

> " When JHVH brought back those that returned to Zion,
> We were like unto them that dream.
> Then was our mouth filled with laughter,
> And our tongue with singing " (Ps. 126[1, 2]).

They brought with them the sacred vessels of
the destroyed Temple ; and the mandate of
Cyrus, authorising their return, required that the
house of God should be restored.   Sacrifice could

be offered on the ancient altar, although the walls of the sanctuary were still in ruins ; and this revival of worship seems to have begun immediately. Opposition from their neighbours, bad harvests, and gradual disillusion prevented any further progress with the Temple for sixteen years. It is then that Haggai, who appears to have seen the first Temple, intervened with the voice of prophecy. There were some who quoted Jeremiah's prediction of seventy years' desolation, and who said that " it is not the time for the Lord's house to be rebuilt." Immediate completion would falsify the prediction. Haggai answered that they had made comfortable houses for themselves ; was it right to let their sanctuary remain a ruin ? He argued that drought and poor harvests were a proper return for the niggardliness of their offerings to God. The people began to work ; and when they were finding it hard to persevere with a good resolution, he gave them encouragement. He admitted it would be impossible to make this Temple like Solomon's, " exceeding magnifical " ; but the Spirit of JHVH would be with them, as it was after the first Exodus from Egypt. There would be international upheavals, but " in this place will I give peace." An opinion of the priests is cited on a casuistical point. If disease is infectious, is health also infectious ? No. Therefore, contact with a dead body unfits a man for every sacred duty. So with a ruined Temple in their midst, their primary religious duty is unfulfilled ; and everything else they do is contaminated. Stimulated by the two prophets, the exiles completed the Temple which, as it ultimately happened, had been seventy years in ruins.

Post-exilic prophecy. The prophetic religion has here assumed a different form from that in which it spoke from Amos to the Second Isaiah. A religion which is superior to time and place, which looks upon all external conditions—temple, land, laws, customs—as negligible accidents, was too lofty for the present condition of the new Jerusalem. The ideal future of the whole world had to give way to the urgency of self-preservation. At the most they might preserve the rudimentary forms of religious expression which had been familiar to their grandfathers. " The heaven is my throne, and the earth is my footstool ; what manner of house will ye build unto me ? " (Isa. 66^1). In spite of this, it is the prophet Haggai who takes the lead in demanding the Temple as a vital necessity for their faith. In appealing to the reward of temporal comfort as an incentive to religious duty, he falls below the prophetic level. His interest in the Gentiles is that their warlike commotions may bring their treasures to adorn the new Temple.

Help from exiles under Persia. For the next sixty years (520–460 B.C.) little is known of Jerusalem. But for one generation we have vivid accounts of the temper and troubles of the religious community. The last of the prophets, called Malachi, and the memoirs of Ezra and Nehemiah, included in the books that bear their name, give contemporary information on the state of religion. The hopes of happiness of fifty years ago had not been fulfilled. The period of reconstruction had proved toilsome and disappointing. The Hebrews who had remained in exile had been much more prosperous, and were able to send substantial gifts to their struggling compatriots. The exiles had wealth and wit, and used both to conciliate the Persian kings; and they were able to intervene successfully in matters of high policy. The Persians disdained the use of temples and altars for the exercise of the spirit, and in this particular they would sympathise with Hebrew dislike of Chaldæan idolatry. Even if the proclamations of Cyrus, Darius, and Artaxerxes, which have been preserved in the Bible, have been freely translated or paraphrased by a Hebrew editor, there is evidence enough to show the friendly attitude of Persia to Jerusalem. The treatment of the Jews at Elephantine in Egypt shows similar friendliness from Cambyses.

Ezra. By diplomatic skill Ezra and Nehemiah obtained important mandates from the Persian kings, and were allowed to come to the assistance of Jerusalem. After a four months' journey Ezra arrived at Jerusalem with a large company of zealous recruits and also material contributions. He "had set his heart to seek the law of the Lord and to do it, and to teach in Israel statutes and judgments." He is also described as "a ready scribe in the Law of Moses." He was of priestly descent, and fourteen ancestors are named among those who connect him with Aaron. The Law of Moses established by Ezra was the Pentateuch in much the same form as we have it in the English Bible. The priest who was expelled by Nehemiah may have taken this Law with him to Samaria; and the Samaritan Pentateuch includes all our sources. The disciples of Ezekiel in Chaldæa and scholars who followed, like Ezra, had produced the Priests' Code; and a harmony of the earlier editions of the Mosaic Code had been compiled into the Five Fifths of the Law. Ezra held a General Assembly of the people, and read and explained the Torah he had brought. The people assented to the Law, and the Pentateuch now acquired in a fuller degree the authority which had been given to Deuteronomy in the reformation of King Josiah (622 B.C.)

Mixed marriages. The most important regulation made by Ezra was the prohibition of inter-marriage between Jews and Gentiles. Though marriage with foreigners was abnormal among contemporary races generally, there was no rigid prohibition on the subject. Ezra so interpreted the idea of a " holy seed " that he strictly forbade Hebrews to marry any other race. The rule was enforced at once, and wives of foreign race had to be divorced. Over a hundred of the priests and many of the laity had made mixed marriages, and the severance caused much sadness. It is possible that the story of Ruth may have been written to mitigate the harshness of this race feeling. Ruth had belonged to Moab, had come to Bethlehem with the purest motives, and had been blessed with King David as one of her descendants. This measure of Ezra made race a vital element in Jewish religion, and erected a wall of separation which still stands between Judaism and humanity.

Nehemiah. About the same time Nehemiah left his office in the Persian Court at Shushan and continued the work of Ezra at Jerusalem. He did not feel that right should go unarmed in this world, that the Holy City should despise defences against unfriendly neighbours. The prophet Zechariah had been urgent to build the Temple ; he had thought no material walls would be necessary. Sparta had built no wall, because she trusted to the valour of her defenders. It was not as an end in itself that Nehemiah wished for a safe city, but that the people might be free to carry out the Law. In spite of internal despondency, in spite of active opposition from Samaritans, Ammonites, and Arabians, by constraining even goldsmiths and apothecaries to act as masons and sentries, he succeeded in quickly completing the walls and the gates. Within the new walls the city was wide and large, but the people were few. Nehemiah concluded that a capital city should contain one-tenth of the country's population, and he made arrangements for drawing select families from the villages. Any flaw in genealogy was reckoned a sufficient reason for exclusion. Children of alien mothers who could not speak the language of the Jews were sternly corrected. The Sabbath law was made more rigid ; by sunset on Friday evening the city gates were shut, and Tyrian fishmongers were not admitted till the Sabbath was past. The laws of tithe, first-fruits, daily sacrifices, supplies of fuel for burnt-offerings, the sacred year, annual subscription for the support of the Temple services, were systematically applied. Surprise has been expressed that any community should submit itself to a discipline so pervasive and exacting ; and it has been suggested as a partial explanation that Western Asia had at the time a general inclination to hierocracy. But it is clear that the great personalities of both Ezra and Nehemiah gave a new vitality to Jerusalem. Their combined influence created the outward forms which were to express and sustain Hebrew religion for several centuries.

Prophecy according to " Malachi." To what extent do the ideals of the great prophets survive in the Holy City of Ezra and Nehemiah ? Their contemporary Malachi has to ignore the conversion of mankind ; his concern is to cure the distemper among his neighbours. The priests, who ought to know better, get rid of blemished animals by using them for Temple sacrifices. Would they dare to offer damaged coinage to their Satrap ? Will a man rob (or defraud) God ? Has the favour of JHVH brought any good to His worshippers ? " Compare your lot with that of Edom " is the answer of the prophet. Piety does not bring any profit, they object ; impiety will bring painful punishment, answers the prophet. They had drought, locusts, bad crops ; are not these the natural returns for their scanty and blemished offerings to the Temple ? The insolent contemn God, and they escape all penalties. Though the rewards for serving God are not immediately apparent, there will come a day when the service of the right will be vindicated.

In this anonymous fragment of prophecy, question and answer, statement and contradiction, are used as in the schools of the scribes of later centuries. Inspiration is replaced by argument and menace ; ritual is a means of cultivating the temperament which the great prophet felt to be swift, irresistible, like lightning, as a fire in their bones. They are all conscious of living on a lower level than they had done in the glorious past. There is no open vision, and naturally they treasure and magnify the great visions of better days. By contrast with their languid present, the message of Moses and the prophets seems to belong to a heroic age ; and the noblest spirits of the time strove to conserve the sense of loyalty to JHVH and His Law. But the public prayers show that the attributes of the One Spiritual God are still reverently apprehended ; and the moral sense is sound. Nehemiah's disdain of bribes, his self-denying

service of his people—which he is not ashamed
to advertise—his indignation at the usury which
would drive a brother into slavery, show that he
felt, as Amos felt, that inhumanity was abhorrent
to JHVH.   Malachi pleaded that all Israel have
a common Father, and are therefore bound in
honour to live as brothers.

Prophets inspire scholars.   The religion as established by Ezra
and Nehemiah included the results of
prophetic inspiration applied to the
interpretation of the past.   Early in the Exile
Ezekiel began to write his discourses ; and he
gives the month and day for all his studies.   He
foresees a return to Jerusalem, and gives an
architect's dream of the dimensions and furniture
of a Utopian sanctuary.   He encourages the
tendency to give a systematic account of the
distant past and to supply a pervasive chrono-
logical scheme.   The use of numbers seems to
have introduced the charm of definite precision
among the disciples of Ezekiel.   This school
created the elaborate specifications for the structure called the Tabernacle ; and in defiance of
transport difficulties the scholars suggested that
it had been carried from station to station in
the wilderness.   The dimensions of Noah's ark,
the ages of the antediluvians, the estimates of the
adult manhood of Israel—600,000 at the Exodus

—are due to the delight of the writers in giving precision to their picture of the past.

The beginning of the world. The desire to understand the past could not avoid asking the question how the world began ? The Spirit of the Living God was so vividly present in the souls of Amos, Hosea, and Isaiah that they were indifferent to the origin or dissolution of the material universe. When inspiration was less intense, reflection and mental effort looked backward into origins. The Second Isaiah had both inspiration and reflection, and he recognised JHVH as the fountain of life and the author of all being. In Chaldæa this prophet might hear stories of a time when there were no men, no names for things above or below, when no gods had yet come into being. Mythology began by giving the birth-story of gods and goddesses, their conflicts and rivalries. But for Isaiah there was no conceivable being prior to the Spirit that had given his soul its clear light. " Before me there was no God formed, neither shall there be after me. I, even I, am JHVH " (Isa. 43^{10}). He rejects Persian ideas of an eternal struggle between Light and Darkness. He takes no notice of any pre-existent raw material, of any primeval chaos. "I am JHVH, and there is none else. I form the light, and create darkness " (Isa. $45^{6, 7}$).

It is to this prophet that the writer of the first chapter in Genesis owes his fundamental ideas.

Gen. 1 and Isaiah of the Exile.

The Hebrew monotheists had many theories thrust on their notice. Apart from recent intercourse with Chaldæa and Persia, their ancestors had come from Mesopotamia, where stories of the Flood and Creation had existed from the earliest times. Cuneiform writing had been used in Palestine before the Hebrews settled there. One of their own kings, Manasseh, had introduced star worship from Assyria, had made altars and chariots for the worship of the heavenly host. The Chaldæan " Genesis " of recent discovery was doubtless circulating in many grotesque forms when this singular Hebrew, the author of the first chapter of Genesis, essayed to diagnose the monstrous phantoms of primeval darkness. But even if we can discern the sources of the amorphous raw material which he used, that should not blind us to the remarkable achievement of the chapter with which our Bible begins. This writer offers no incantation to lay old dragons underground ; he condenses the geology, botany, and zoology of his time, and gives them their place in his picture of the creative process. But when he looks away from man's home to the heavens, his caution has to be vigilant. To describe the birth of the universe he had to use words which were already saturated with superstition and fatal error. " Chaos," " Tehom "—" the great deep," " brooding," " sun," " moon ": each of these terms had age-long associations with polydæmon-**Sun-** ism. The Sun had commanded almost **worship.** universal adoration from the greatest races for millenniums. His sanctuaries had name and fame, from Heliopolis to Stonehenge, from Beth-shemesh to Babylon. Even in Athens at her brightest the higher criticism of the Moon's divinity had proved intolerable to the city of intellectual light. Among his own people also there still prevailed a secret desire to keep friendly with Sun and Moon.

> "If," said Job, "I beheld the sun when it shined,
>   Or the moon walking in brightness;
>   And my heart hath been secretly enticed,
>   And my mouth hath kissed my hand,"

this were an iniquity deserving to be punished by the judges (Job 31$^{26. 27}$). The Jewish refugees in Egypt defied the censure of Jeremiah, and renewed their devotion to the Queen of heaven, " We will certainly perform every word that is gone forth out of our mouth, to burn incense unto the queen of heaven, and to pour out drink offerings unto her, as we have done, we and our fathers, our kings and our princes,

in the cities of Judah, and in the streets of
Jerusalem: for then had we plenty of victuals,
and were well, and saw no evil" (Jer. 44^{17}). Not
only in popular custom, but in their sacred
Scripture there were doctrines of creation which
required revision. The Judæan story which
told how Adam was made from the moistened
earth and put into Eden, how the trees and
animals were produced for his entertainment,
and how, finally, Eve was formed while Adam was
asleep, how they disobeyed the command and
were expelled to endure the hardships of life—
that story had been familiar to every Hebrew
for centuries. The author of the cosmogony
in the first chapter of Genesis (Gen. 1^1–2^4) had
revised the Judæan story of the Flood. He also
desires to supersede the poetic elements of Eden
and Eve ; using more austere words—" create "
for " mould," " make," " fashion," he ascribes
the result to the voice rather than the hand of
the Creator. " Male and female created he
them." There is no separate act for the origin
of woman. The Judæan story takes no notice
of the stars ; but the later writer must. He does
not dare to name the sun or moon. They had
been deities for all the world, and to use their
names would imply too much recognition of their
character. With resolute rationalism, with what

must have seemed to many a blasphemous utilitarianism, he dethrones the solar and lunar deities and prescribes their proper function: " let them be for luminaries " by day and by night; let them serve as chronometers for mankind. To our own day there remain some who speak of Sabbath rather than of Sunday; there are also those who feel that their worship is faulty unless their sanctuary is built to meet the rising sun, in the correct eastward position. Both parties would be perfectly understood by the author of the preface to Genesis. A hundred generations have been the happier for this man's courageous adventure among primeval mysteries. Soon after his day the Psalms could call upon sun, moon, and stars to join in singing a *Te Deum* in honour of the Creator.

What is man? The prophetic conception of God as One, Spiritual, and Holy, has been faithfully preserved in the chapter on Creation; How does this writer regard man? Of all things that men see, stones, stars, flowers, living creatures, the greatest is what at first escapes notice—man himself. When self-study begins, it is the soul that startles man more than the body. Any one who has dreamed a dream is aware of vivid visions which are real though incorporeal. The nature of spirit is perplexing; but spirit has

dominion over the things it creates, and the
Spirit that created the world must be the Supreme
reality. If we are to learn the nature of God it
will not be from inferior things—inorganic or
sub-human—but from the highest known to us,
the Soul. Hence the higher humanism is the
foundation for theism. In the self or soul there
is a kinship with God; it was pronounced good
in the Divine intention, and was created in the
likeness of God. It is greater than the Sun, and
must not worship the Sun. In this particular
the doctrine is in accord with the experience of
the prophets.

Ideals in practice. But the chief merit in the Priests'
Code, to which Genesis I is the preface,
is its skill in bringing sublime ideas into contact
with the humblest human capacity. The spring
and autumn festivals were invested with lessons
from history, which children and slaves learned
with pleasure. The dietary customs were ascribed
to definite occasions in history, and in addition
to being sound on hygienic grounds they confirmed an affectionate loyalty to their fathers.
Why did they abstain from eating animal food
unless the blood had been carefully drained away?
Because long ago the earth had filled itself with
cruelty—of man to man, and man to beast—
and the Deluge was allowed as a punishment.

All Noah's descendants should keep this regulation ; but the nations have forgotten the precepts
of Noah.   So, too, the picture of Creation is not
left in the region of lofty speculation.   In hot
climates it is easy to rest and hard to labour.
Yet the Hebrews have to be expressly commanded
to cease work.   They have to complete their work
in six days ; but the seventh is sacred to the
Creator.   " In it thou shalt not do any work,
thou nor thy son, nor thy daughter, thy bondman, nor thy bondwoman, nor thy cattle, nor thy
stranger that is within thy gates."   The Sabbath
is, according to the Law, of supreme importance
in cultivating a religious temperament, and it is
therefore invested with the highest sanction.

Hymn-book of the Second Temple.   The greatest service rendered to the
world by the worshippers in the Second
Temple was the production of the
Psalms.   Though half the Psalter is connected
with the name of David—as the patron of music
and poetry—it is clear that most of the Psalms
were composed after the Exile.   It was for use
in the public worship of the post-exilic period
that the Psalms were collected into groups of
sacred songs.   These poems were not made to
order ; nor did their writers think of the influence
their meditations were to exercise in the future.
They all gave glad obedience to the Law.   They

lived in communion with the righteous God of the prophets; they were concerned about fulfilling the moral rather than the ceremonial requirements of the Law. Without intending or expecting to acquire fame, these writers were honest and sincere in their own deepest feelings. Others felt their sincerity and shared their devotion. Some experience of the heart was faithfully mirrored in a psalm by a solitary soul. Other men in like perplexity were helped by the Psalm to understand themselves, to master their emotions, and to share the resignation or adoration of the author. When united to appropriate music and sung in sacred assemblies, the Psalms created a common temperament which gained intensity from numbers and changed assemblies into congregations. In the Psalter may be found slight and occasional traces of narrowness, such as a vindictive feeling toward enemies, an inhospitable attitude to Gentiles, a claim for prosperity as a reward for piety; but in general the Psalms are nearly as free from selfish particularism as the axioms of Euclid. The names of the authors have been forgotten, the historical situations in which they were composed can rarely be identified. Wherever men feel sorrow, penitence, perplexity, or hope, they can be guided to feel confidence, reverence, and adoration through communion with God. The fact that the Christian Church has been able to adopt this Hebrew Hymnary is a testimony to its genuinely catholic character.

Alexander the Great. The little school of religion in Jerusalem, while busy composing Psalms and cosmogonies, could not avoid entanglement with the great powers of this world. Persia had been supreme for two centuries (536–330 B.C.), and gave place to Alexander the Great. The Balkans had produced a small army and a great leader who in ten years (334–323 B.C.) conquered all that was known of Asia and Africa. He differed from previous conquerors by importing ideas, by tolerating the religions of the vanquished, and by founding cities such as Alexandria and Sekunderabad. He raised the grade of material civilisation and disseminated some elements of Greek culture. The spirit of the nations might be well compared to the animals of a menagerie, and the seer who wrote the book of Daniel thought of Alexander as a leopard equipped with four wings. Though Tyre and Gaza resisted and suffered severely, Jerusalem had little trouble in making terms with the Macedonian conqueror. The tribute paid to Persia was continued to the new governor, who considerately allowed the Sabbatical year to be free from taxation.

The name of Alexander has been kept familiar by his selection of a site for a great city—Alexandria. He required to attract population, and invited Jewish immigrants, who were to have equal rights with colonists from Macedonia. Within a single generation a Jewish quarter of the city had acquired influence, and the export of grain to Rome yielded the Jews good profits in transport. Within a century they had been fruitful and had multiplied to a million, according to a generous estimate. They had learned Greek and had forgotten their original Hebrew. They required a Greek version of their Holy Scripture ; and the Law of Moses appeared in the Greek translation, called by the name of the Septuagint. As a language Greek has been justly described as " musical and prolific, giving a soul to objects of sense and a body to the abstractions of philosophy." By this time Hebrew was known to few ; even in Palestine it was like a little island surrounded by a sea of Aramaic. The laity of Jerusalem had difficulty in understanding the Hebrew of the Law and the Prophets : the reader in the synagogue had to give a paraphrase or Targum, verse by verse, in Aramaic. No doubt a similar paraphrase into Greek had been customary in Egypt; and the expounder may have

The Scripture in Greek.

been tempted to expand the sacred text and have thus furnished an impetus to pulpit oratory. To have the Bible in Greek meant that the Hebrew wisdom gleaned from a millennium was accessible to the most enlightened section of the human race.

Meeting of Greek and Hebrew thought. Contact with the Greeks meant also that Hebrew wisdom had to measure itself against something great. Conquest and coercion could not tempt Hebrews to believe in the absurd idolatry of the Chaldæans. But Greece had also studied life, and by clear-eyed intelligence had discovered beauty as well as truth. Greece had a literature and Hebrews learned to read Plato. In Alexandria the interaction of Greek and Hebrew thought produced much noble literature, which found a place in the Greek Bible, although it was excluded from the Hebrew Canonical Scriptures. Even in Palestine there were many Jews who found the easy morals and picturesque customs of their suzerains more acceptable than the Puritanism of their ancestral religion. New cities with Greek colonists grew up in Palestine ; and these were equipped with a racecourse and theatre. Many Hebrews adopted Greek names and competed in the athletic sports. Even in the priesthood the competition for the office of high priest led to shameful betrayals of religious fidelity to Mosaic

Law. The Jews who favoured Hellenist culture were often in a majority ; and if peaceful penetration had been allowed to work inoffensively, the stern Puritan party—the Hasidim—might have contracted into a small sect.

Israel and the den of lions. It was under Antiochus Epiphanes, the ruler of Syria (175–164 B.C.) that Hebrew faith had to pass through the fiery furnace. This monarch had spent thirteen years of his youth in Rome. He had been sent there by his father as a guarantee that the heavy tribute imposed on Syria by the Romans would be duly paid. In Rome this youth had learned to scoff at every kind of religious scruple ; the best thing he found to take back to Antioch with him was a group of Roman gladiators. He was always short of money, and raised revenue by selling the high priest's office to a mercenary candidate, Menelaus. To effect this he had to contrive the death of the legitimate high priest, who had sought sanctuary in a temple of Apollo. He had also to insult the Judæans by appointing one who was of non-priestly descent. The Judæans were shocked by these crimes, and Menelaus was left with an empty Temple and general hostility. As a remedy Menelaus agreed to the abolition of Hebrew religion altogether. The Law of Moses, he suggested, taught hatred to humanity, inhospitality to strangers, and made conviviality impossible. He encouraged Antiochus to exercise his power in establishing Hellenic religion. Penalties were imposed for Sabbath observance, circumcision, refusal to eat forbidden fruit. The Temple was furnished with a statue of Zeus ; unclean swine were offered in sacrifice ; and copies of the Law were burned. Similar regulations were enforced in the country villages. The mass of the people sullenly acquiesced ; some expected miraculous Divine intervention, others approved the policy of Menelaus, would no one dare to resist the ungodly Power ?

The Maccabees. In the town of Modin a Syrian officer and his Judæan adjutant arrived to secure the conformity of the people to the new ritual. An old man, Mattathias, and his five sons openly defied the authorities. " If all the people in the kingdom obeyed the order of the monarch, to depart from the faith of their fathers, I and my sons would abide by the covenant of our forefathers." A Judæan who went forward to conform was killed on the spot, and the Syrian officer shared his fate. Resistance had begun, adherents were attracted for the defence of the Law and the Covenant. By skilful guerilla warfare the sons of Mattathias gained battle after battle, and in the end they delivered Jerusalem and Judah from the yoke of the foreigner. The book about Daniel was written during the struggle, to inspire the Maccabees with fidelity and hope. The Temple was purified and reconsecrated after being polluted by the " abomination of desolation." The " two thousand three hundred evenings and mornings," " the time, times and an-half " indicate the interval between the desecration and reconsecration of the Temple (July 168 B.C.–November 165 B.C.).

Judæa independent. By good fortune the successors of the victorious Covenanters were enabled to secure political independence and prosperity for Judæa for almost a century. In 142 B.C. they began a new era and reckoned time from the first " Year of the High Priest, Commander of the Army and Prince of the Nation." They coined their own money, inscribing on the one side of the coins " Shekel of Israel " and on the obverse " Jerusalem the Holy." But they knew that the great prophets had hoped for something nobler than they had yet attained. They would not give the title of king to Simon, for only one of the house and lineage of David was entitled to be called King of the Jews. It was provided that the sovereign power should belong to the prince, or Nasi, only until the appearance of the true prophet Elijah, who would be the forerunner of the Messiah. The first Nasi, Simon, anxious for the future, invited the alliance of Rome, which in time sent Pompey and Vespasian to end the secular sovereignty of Judæa.

Government by consent. One of the undesigned results of religious life under the Second Temple was to suggest a workable relation of the spiritual and temporal powers in a community. It is often said that Judah had been a nation before the Captivity, but after the Exile she became a Church. Except for a brief interval, the Hebrews lived under foreign sovereignty with an alien creed. The Mosaic Law had to be put in practice by a religious fellowship which did not enjoy secular independence. " As for the land," says Nehemiah, " that thou gavest to our fathers to eat the fruit thereof and the good thereof, behold, we are servants in it. And it yieldeth much increase unto the kings whom thou didst set over us because of our sins : also they have power over our bodies, and over our cattle, at their pleasure " (Neh. 9[36, 37]). Temporal governments had in these circumstances to be conciliated, and there was no hope of coercion by force. It was further impossible to secure the adherence of their own people by the use of the secular arm. Nations can be tested by the class which they agree to consider aristocratic. In this community it was the priesthood which was selected for hereditary honours. Though their authority became very powerful, it rested not on force but on government by consent. And there was a law which was read aloud every week to the humblest of the congregation, and which made arbitrary governance impossible. The tithes and dues that were given for the maintenance of worship were given by voluntary consent. The power of communal opinion was more effective to this end than any decree of Cyrus or Alexander the Great could have been. From this adjustment of sacred and secular duty the Church inherited the feeling that the Roman Empire had to be converted and ought not to be coerced. In later centuries the Law is tacitly accepted, and the problem how to apply it fairly, exercises the ingenuity of Charlemagne and of Gustavus Adolphus. Sovereign force is no necessity to a religion ; secular independence in a national form may even be a hindrance to the right disposition of the soul. It is one of the compensations for the long subordination of post-exilic Jerusalem, that the world is ready to believe that a man can be good and can serve God wherever his house may be. Nor can spiritual obligations be disannulled by any temporal power, whether by Imperial Decree or by a democratic majority.

Inherited sin. Another specimen of the growth of a fixed opinion may be seen in the later conception of Sin. It had become a common belief that the land of promise was an essential in religion. Failure to observe the Law involved banishment from the Holy Land as its express penalty. Double expiation for admitted sins had been followed by penitence and restoration from Babylon. The course of Hebrew history, begun in servitude, had continued in struggles for independence and ended in Exile. Thus the sense of sin, the admission of guilt, and the necessity for atonement had forced itself into the interpretation of history. From Hebrew history this sense of Sin was extended to the history of other nations and even to human nature in general. The anticipation of failure, the impossibility of moral success, the *non posse non peccare* had come to be regarded as the surest and saddest element in human nature. Depravity is original and innate ; " every imagination of the thoughts of man's heart is only evil continually " (Gen. 6⁵). The Deluge had been permitted long ago because men were wicked. The hardship which men endure in procuring their food, the pains of childbirth, are proof enough that the human race are doing penal servitude for their crimes in the past. Other nations with entirely different histories could not transfer the teachings of Hebrew history and apply them to their own different experience. But the Hebrews had come to consider this lesson as above criticism. There was a deep desire for deliverance from this despairing dogma of impotence. Rabbinic doctrine held that the Messiah, a descendant of the house of David, would come and restore the kingdom of Israel, which under his sceptre would extend over the whole world. The evangelist wrote of another : " Thou shalt call his name Jesus : for he shall save his people from their sins " (Matt. 1²¹).

LECTURE III.

Judaism.

THE Old and New Testaments in our English Bible are separated in time by an interval of two hundred years. From the crisis when Israel was delivered from the den of lions, when her spirit walked free amid the flames of the fiery furnace—as told in the book about Daniel—till the day when St. Paul wrote a letter to a few Christians at Salonika (165 B.C.– 50 A.D.), the Bible found nothing worthy of preservation for its readers. The Greek Bible was more hospitable than the Hebrew, and admitted the books called the Apocrypha to the rank of useful reading. But beyond this wider library there was a copious literature ; and the secular annals of these two centuries reveal in the Hebrew character 'a darker side of stern ferocity, of grim power for evil as well as for good, which the Bible decided to ignore. It is the Hebrew spirit at its best which meets us in both Testaments.

77

What makes a nation truly great ? Deuteronomy replies, " What great nation is there that hath statutes and judgments so righteous as all this law ? " (Deut. 4^8). They had in Deuteronomy a code with noble elements, mingling justice with humanity ; and they needed neither to go over the seas nor into the sky to discover their duty. Did this good Law make the Hebrews any better than their contemporaries in the period between the Testaments ? The records of the time show that their own domestic dissensions, their jealousies, their struggles for high office, the strife of religious factions, wrought untold harm to the community and made their righteous statutes ineffectual. A few instances will illustrate the combination of high ideals with low achievement. The Temple was regarded as unspeakably holy ; the foot of a foreigner introduced profanation. The Persian eunuch Bagoas, long before the most intense period, had been warned that he would pollute the sacred area if he dared to enter. He inquired whether he was not as pure as the son of the high priest who had been murdered by a brother in the Holy Place. Again we find that in the year 95 B.C. Alexander Jannæus was officiating as high priest while celebrating the Feast of Tabernacles.

He had to pour out a vessel of water, as part of the ritual; and by doing his office in the wrong way, he offended the scruples of the Pharisees. His action caused a riot among the Temple-worshippers, with 4000 fatal casualties, and was followed by six years of violent civil war between Pharisees and Sadducees. The same Jannæus resented the Pharisaic criticism of his right to his position, and had 800 Pharisees crucified in a single day. Some 10,000 Pharisees had to flee from their home and fellow-countrymen to find refuge in Syria and Egypt. About the same time Simeon ben Shetach, brother of Queen Salome, acquired fame as a patron of learning, and did much to revive the glory of the Law. His inexorable adherence to legal form made him insist on the execution of his own son, who had been regularly tried and condemned on evidence which, before the execution, was admitted to be false. During Simeon's visit to Ascalon it was proved to his satisfaction that eighty women had been guilty of witchcraft; and the wisest Pharisee of his day condemned these eighty women to death by crucifixion. One other instance of grim resolution may be cited from the capture of the hill-fortress Masada. The garrison consisted of 1000 Zealots with their wives and children, and they made a brave defence.   When it became clear that the Romans must conquer, the garrison decided to kill their wives and children and to die by their own hands rather than be taken alive.   When the Romans entered the fortress they found only two women and five children, who came creeping out from a cave.   The temper which has been found among good soldiers in the worst of situations was not wanting in Judæa.   It was not among weaklings and cowards that the religion of the scribes and Pharisees and Apostles had its being.

Judaism.   Judaism may be used as a name for that form of Hebrew religion which made self-preservation its chief end, and which definitely rejected the evangelic invitation to convert the Gentiles.   In the days of Pontius Pilate, about the beginning of the Christian era, the Hebrews had a fair chance of becoming the directors of human history.   A reasonable religion and sound morals had kept the race alive, when Philistines, Assyrians, Ammonites and others were disappearing.   Moreover, the " remnant " of the Captivity had been fruitful and had mul- tiplied a hundredfold in five centuries.   The Hebrews had been carefully bred since the days of Ezra ; they had settled in centres of wealth, enterprise, and intelligence.   They were well placed for diffusing higher conceptions of God and duty among their contemporaries. Greek mythology had lost its hold on popular belief; philosophy appealed only to the few; and curiosity made any fantastic foreign religion welcome and easily credible. In many cases thoughtful Gentiles frequented the synagogues, and listened with serious interest to the Law and the Prophets. Had Herod the Great or Agrippa, with their official power, possessed the wisdom of Ecclesiasticus, a friendly interfusion of Hebrew and Hellenic wisdom might have captivated the Roman Empire. But Herod and Agrippa were mainly concerned in the defence and aggrandisement of their secular power; and as a nation the Hebrews disdained the missionary career and, like other nations, they decided to fight for their own independence. Suppose any nation has perfect internal health, with every prospect of having its material needs supplied, with surplus energy free to use in new directions, it would be reasonable to hope that such a nation might decide that the best way to use energy and mind is to study the world and the nature of man, to banish disease and misery, to cultivate goodwill and universal brotherhood. Yet such a nation would be exceptional in modern as well as in ancient times. Teutons, Gauls, Britons, Parthians fought for independence whenever

6

they had a fair chance ; why should Judæa remain subject to Cæsar ? The axioms of antiquity, the practice of nations, the dominant influences in history, have blindly accepted sovereign independence as the chief end of a nation. In the case of Judæa the fight was not merely for home, but also for religion ; patriotism gained intensity from the sanctity they attached to the Holy Land.

Judæa under Rome. Rome had registered the population amid intense indignation, and methodically collected her taxes from all the inhabitants of Palestine. The procurators and centurions often irritated and sometimes tried to soothe the religious susceptibilities of the Jews. The presence of a statue in a synagogue, of the picture of an eagle near the Temple, the demand for new bread on Saturdays, disrespect shown to a Roll of the Law, were enough to cause riots. The death of Caligula in 41 A.D. had relieved one dangerous situation. Claudius was more considerate, and Nero, *qualis artifex*, was too busy playing and posturing to attend to complaints against his procurators in Palestine. Jewish discontent grew in strength and method. There were irreconcilables—the Zealots—who preferred death to subjection to Rome ; extremist Zealots —Sicarii—who carried daggers and practised assassination for private vengeance or personal gain. The Pharisees, who formed the mass of moderate opinion, were often maddened by insults to their religion. Only a few like Berenice and Flavius Josephus were aware of the strength of Rome; but even the worldly Sadducee might see a reasonable chance of successful war. With a population roughly estimated at two millions in Palestine and as many more dispersed in important cities, the number of Jews would be little short of the total of Romans, with pure descent. Moreover, all parties were touched by the vague hope of Messianic help and consequent world dominance.

Fall of Jerusalem, 70 A.D. The war for Jewish independence began in Galilee in 66 A.D. and ended four years later with the capture of Jerusalem by the Romans. This result was due, not so much to the valour of the Romans as to the savage strife of discordant factions among the defenders. The national energy and mind had spent itself in vain in this appeal to the sword. The natural man, however, can hardly blame the grandsons of the defenders of Jerusalem for making another struggle for national freedom.

The world's happiest years. To see in right perspective the story of the Hebrews, we must note the condition of the world in general. The Roman Empire had acquired sovereignty over the accessible parts of the earth, and maintained universal order with an army and navy of less than half a million men. " By every honourable expedient," says Gibbon, " the emperors Hadrian and the two Antonines invited the friendship of the barbarians ; and endeavoured to convince mankind that the Roman power, raised above the temptation of conquest, was actuated only by the love of order and justice " (*Decline,* ch. i.).

" If a man," says the same great historian, " were called to fix the period in the history of the world during which the condition of the human race was most happy and prosperous, he would, without hesitation, name that which elapsed from the death of Domitian to the accession of Commodus (*i.e.* 96–161 A.D.). The vast extent of the Roman empire was governed by absolute power under the guidance of virtue and wisdom " (Gibbon, ch. iii.).

The best was past for Judæa. The records of Judæa for this period form a sorrowful exception to this universal rule. When Titus was delivering his final assaults on Jerusalem, Johanan ben Zakkai, one of the wisest members of the Sanhedrim, who had pleaded in vain for conciliation, pretended to have died and had himself conveyed as a corpse through the sentries of the Zealots, and made terms with the Romans. He gathered a school at Jamnia on the coast near Joppa, and provided a home for the remnants of the Holy Synod after Jerusalem was destroyed. From this new centre the Rabbis exercised a spiritual governance over their brethren scattered abroad. A great scholar joined them in Akība, who formulated pervasive principles for classifying the manifold topics of the Oral Law, and thus lightened the burden of the unwritten Mishna on the memory of the scholars. They also encouraged the wealthy proselyte, Aquila of Pontus, to make a fresh literal translation of the Hebrew Bible to replace the Septuagint Version, which was too favourable to Christians in the old prophecies concerning Christ. These scholars of Jamnia also formulated a strict defence against Christianity. They forbade intercourse with Christians and Pagans, introduced a curse into their prayers, and ordered the Christian books to be burned. They also determined finally the books which were to have a place in the Old Testament, excluding the Apocrypha and admitting, after considerable debate, the books of Canticles and Ecclesiastes.

Nostalgia. Though thus diligent in study and in the practice of religion, Judaism was not yet reconciled to the loss of the Holy City.

Other tribes fought for independence, and Jews could not be blamed for their desire of freedom. But their own best advisers had always warned them that their supreme good was something higher than national independence. Jeremiah had told them so in the time of the Chaldæans, but he had been disregarded and disaster followed. In the generation before Titus they had been told that non-resistance would prove best in the end (Matt. 5^{39}), that it was quite possible to serve God faithfully under Cæsar. Now once again under the Emperor Hadrian (130–135 A.D.) their own religious guides strove for conciliation, and again in vain. Conscious of the Divine mandate to evangelise the world, the Prophets had seen that even successful war against the great powers would not advance the true religion. But the common national ambition of the Gentiles appealed more strongly to the Hebrews than the peculiar mission they had inherited. So, for national independence and perhaps for world sovereignty, they again appealed to the sword and went to war with the Roman Empire.

Bar Kochba's rebellion. An adventurous leader—Bar Koziba by name—arose for the occasion, and was accepted by the profound scholar Akība as a Messianic king, with the nobler title Bar Kochba—Son of a Star. Combined action was arranged between the Jewish communities in Cyrene, Egypt, Cyprus, and Babylon, and even the Samaritans assisted the Palestinians. Hadrian's visit to Judæa in 130 A.D., and his proposal to rebuild Jerusalem as a Pagan city, sufficed to set the insurrection ablaze. According to the computation of a Jewish historian, Bar Kochba mustered about 400,000 troops, not far short of the scattered total of Rome. There was more chance of religious freedom under Rome than there had been under Assyria, Chaldæa, or the successors of Alexander the Great. In this case it was not a war for toleration ; there was some ground, apart from the Messianic hope, for regarding this resistance as a bid for world-power.

In Cyrene the Jewish troops are said to have slaughtered 200,000 Greeks and Romans ; in Cyprus 240,000, great numbers also in Egypt and Babylon, and in all cases there were reprisals in kind. Cyprus decreed that even a Jew who had suffered shipwreck should never again be allowed to land on the island. In Palestine, Bar Kochba overran the land, slew the Romans, captured fifty forts and hundreds of villages. In token of victory and independence he minted coins with suitable inscriptions, and for two years he was sole sovereign of Palestine. He also punished the Christians who refused to join the war for the possession of Palestine.

Roman victory. Rome could not ignore this grave menace to her power. Her best general, Julius Severus, was summoned from fighting the Britons, who also desired independence. In due time Severus arrived with a Mediterranean Expeditionary Force. His enemy was too powerfully equipped and too skilfully placed to make frontal assault possible. Like Titus, Severus made time his ally. If peasants were in arms they could not till their lands, and want of provisions would tell in a second year. By cautious warfare, by winning in some fifty battles and sieges, Severus drove Bar Kochba and his refugees into his great fortress of Bither, between Jerusalem and the coast. Then followed siege and final defeat. Half a million Jews are said to have perished in this last attempt of Judaism to wield the sceptre of Imperial Cæsar. Again their prophets had been proved to be right, and their fond hopes of national supremacy a fatal illusion.

Julian "the Apostate." Never again after Bar Kochba was Judaism in a position to reconquer Judæa by force of arms. Once it seemed as if a friend were to bring them home again. The honourable Pagan, the Emperor Julian, was anxious to displace Christianity in the Roman

Empire by a purified Paganism with an adequate sacrificial cult. The emperor addressed a letter to his " Brother, the venerable Patriarch Julos (Hillel)," bestowing privileges on all Jews, and offering to rebuild their Temple at his own expense (362 A.D.). Masons were soon at work on the foundations, but a series of portentous explosions and the early death of Julian put an end to this interesting enterprise.

The wandering Jew. The landless Jews, after the loss of Judæa, had now the whole world before them. They were not merely emigrants asking hospitality ; they required permission to observe their own Law and religion. They were not content with the Ten Commandments and the 100th Psalm ; but they had formed strict rules for every detail of life, the Sabbath, New Moons, and annual Festivals, methods of slaughter and of preparing food, synagogues and schools and daily prayers, sacred dues and contributions, endogamy and the duty of protesting against every form of idolatry. They could not settle among strangers without refusing to assimilate ; and their very presence compelled their host to criticise and disturb his own authorised customs. It is little wonder that it took time to secure a licence for the Jewish religion in the Roman Empire ; and it is creditable to the humanity of the ancient world that emigrants with principles so tenaciously held should have been received into so many diverse communities.

Jews among Pagans. Among races which had forgotten their past and had no fixed tradition, the Jews were received with little inconvenience ; and their presence raised the standard of thought and conduct. In many cases they made converts to Judaism. Rulers and their peoples adopted monotheism and retained their new faith for generations. Such were the Queen of Adiabene on the Tigris, Aretas of Nabatæa, and other chiefs in Arabia, Bulan, the prince of the Chazars on the Volga, with four thousand of his nobles. Judaism even penetrated to India, Ceylon, and China ; but beyond mere persistence they made little impression. The Chinese community was recently identified ; and it was found that though it had forgotten nearly all the principles of its religion, it had clung tenaciously to an irrational detail, and was known among the Chinese as the tribe that refused to eat of the sinew that shrank.

Jews pre-ferred cities. There were many empty spaces on the earth nineteen hundred years ago, and it might have been expected that the exiles would have sought for freedom in the solitudes. But the task of subduing the earth to yield her increase, the conflict with thorns and thistles, the hereditary labour required to make the desert blossom as the rose, was repellent to the Jew. Cradled in the Arabian wilderness, haunted with needless horror of the brickmoulder's useful craft, they had enjoyed the land of milk and honey, and had an instinctive preference for civilised life. " Never settle in a place which has not a priest, a teacher, and a doctor " was one of their ancient maxims. It never is easy to transplant those who have lived in cities back to the land. Unoccupied areas accordingly appealed as little to Jews in the first century as the offers in recent times of such places as Mexico, Uganda, or Cyprus. To win what they prized was easier in the cities than in the country ; and so they migrated to the centres of civilisation.

Jews under Rome, Pagan and Christian. In the West, Jews had obtained recognition from Rome before losing Judæa ; and by influence with emperors and officials they maintained freedom for worship and commerce. Scholars like Origen and Jerome got friendly help from Jewish scholars in the study of Hebrew ; but officially Judaism maintained the opposition to the Christian seceders, which it had offered to St. Paul on his missionary journeys. When Constantine the Great made Christianity the official religion of the Roman Empire, the party in power had the difficult task of acknowledging the rights of a minority which denied the fundamentals of the State religion. The Gospels became familiar; and common people, especially at Easter-time, were moved to indignation with the Pharisees, and too easily inclined to visit the sins of the fathers on the children. The authorities in Church and State tried to protect the Jews. Pope Gregory (590–604) wrote a Pastoral Epistle in which he says: "We forbid you to molest the Jews or to restrict them in opposition to the established laws : we further permit them to live as Romans, and to dispose of their property without prejudice ; we only prohibit them from owning Christian slaves." The Council of Toledo (633 A.D.) decreed that Jews should not be driven into Christianity by violence or threats of punishment, but converts were to be held bound by their profession. In Spain and in France the Jews had many centuries of undisturbed prosperity, and produced great scholars and some poets. Queen Judith (840 A.D.) expressed a common feeling when she said that "the Jews ought to be specially honoured by reason of their descent from the patriarchs and prophets." Preaching and persuasion were used to make converts to Christianity ; and some of these converts became the most zealous critics of their kindred. Many

Jews made an outward profession of the dominant faith and secretly continued to practise Judaism. The Crusades embittered feeling in every direction ; Christianity made war on Islam for possession of the Holy Land, and turned with sore severity on the Jews in their own lands. Popular riots caused much bloodshed ; the Church sanctioned severe civil penalties for religious nonconformity. The sad climax of this tendency can be read in the terrible history of the Inquisition in Spain (1490), the tortures of the Marranos, and the banishment of the steadfast Jews. England joined with other European countries in this expulsion ; and the Ottoman Empire gave shelter to many of the refugees from Christian Europe. Under modern democracies citizens may profess any religion which offers no obvious hurt to the common welfare. The conversion of a soul by physical force is now admitted to be impossible, and to be contrary to the nature of religion. The constancy of the Jewish martyrs, in refusing to do even a good thing by force, has been of conspicuous service in teaching the world this important lesson.

Jews and Persians. In the Middle East, Jews encountered Persians. The disposal of the dead was a matter of much concern in that land, and King Shabur (375 A.D.) demanded from the

Rabbi Hama by what authority he buried the dead ? Hama could not quote a verse to settle the question, and was reproached by his colleagues. Yezdegird and his successor (450 A.D.) forbade Sabbath observance, and the Prince of the Hebrew Captivity suffered martyrdom—the first case in Babylonia. Many Jews emigrated to Arabia and India owing to these dissensions.

Jews and Moslems. The rise of Islam (622 A.D.) brought the Jews into conflict with a new Semitic religion. The respect of Mohammed for the Hebrew and Christian Scriptures made him friendly to the Jews ; but controversy engendered hostility ; and the arguments in the Koran had some influence in making Moslem sentiment permanently critical. The Khalif Omar (640 A.D.), desiring to make Arabia entirely Moslem, transferred the Arabian Jews to a district near Kufa on the Euphrates. Arabian philosophy inspired some criticism of the Talmud in Jewish schools. Their common Semitic ancestry and their common loyalty to Abraham made Jews more at home with Moslems than with Western Christians.

Jewish Rationalism. In estimating the spiritual history of Judaism as a whole, it has been claimed that it deserves especial credit for its rationalism, its freedom from apocalypse and mysticism. The mental energy which carried the Mishna by memory for centuries, which created the Twelve Folio Volumes of the Talmud, is certainly impressive. Had the same intellectual power been applied to science, medicine, philosophy, or literature, great results might have been achieved; and Jews like Ibn Gabirol in Spain, or Maimonides in Egypt, who looked beyond their own traditions, were able to illumine the best learning of their age. But Jewish scholars worked on the text, the possible interpretations, literal or allegorical, the traditional applications of the sacrosanct Mosaic Law to the experience of life. Given the Pentateuch with all its inconsistencies as major premiss, the fortunes of Israel as minor, what conclusions can be drawn? If any one wished to express new opinions he had to go back to Methuselah for a *nom-de-plume*. Freedom of speech was possible only for the patriarchs and antediluvians who lived before Moses had revealed the final Law. Even under an ancient name, the author of fiction had to recognise the validity of the Mosaic Law; and the Law was posthumously imposed on the antediluvians and the angels and conceived as preceding Creation. Hence Jewish scholars had to build on the Law, written and oral, and it was exceptional to apply higher criticism to the Law itself. Rabban Chivi (950 A.D.), at Balkh, in Bactria, not only rejected the Talmud, but found two hundred difficulties in the Pentateuch itself. Another scholar, Ben Jasus of Toledo (1050 A.D.), dared to point out that the Dukes of Edom had got a place in Genesis from a late interpolator. Ibn Ezra in his commentary on the Pentateuch (1153 A.D.) enigmatically hints that several verses in the Torah had been added by a later hand, and perhaps the whole was edited long after Moses. These isolated voices had less influence than the remarkable succession of Jewish Protestants, the Karaites, who seceded from Rabbinical Judaism and directed fresh attention to the Pentateuch as alone having Divine authority.

Study of the Law blind to the origin of the Pentateuch. It is a disappointing result of Jewish rationalism that talented scholars should have devoted intense study for fifteen hundred years to a few books without discovering the modern analysis of the Pentateuch into its constituent sources. Had there been any open vision, any independent critical investigation, the truth could not have remained hidden from a scrutiny so intense. But it was the depth of their reverence, their zeal for God, which prevented them from seeing clearly how their Scriptures had been made, how they might be applied more fruitfully to life, without giving rise to a form of Bibliolatry. The Torah remained a sealed book in spite of all the laborious commentaries of successive generations.

Messianic claimants. But creative imagination claims the whole universe as its sphere, and neither the laws of Church nor State can prevent its exercise. There is a freedom inherent to the human mind which no artificial obstacles can fetter. This element in Judaism often displayed its power in defiance of the conscientious rationalism of the schools. The Law and the Prophets encouraged the expectation of a Divine Deliverer in mortal extremity. When they lost their land, the exiles became more loyal to their Law ; yet aliens sometimes made them martyrs. Surely, then, had come the time for the Divine Redeemer ? In such situations there were some, often many, who set their hopes upon any claimant to Messianic honours. A mere enumeration of false Messiahs will show the enduring strength of this hope, and the influence of the Jewish Prayer Book in keeping it alive through the centuries.

In the days of Pontius Pilate a Samaritan claimed to be Messiah, and gathered his adherents on Mount Gerizim, to whom he offered to show the sacred vessels used by Moses. Pilate had the ringleaders executed, and was summoned to Rome to justify his procedure.

Theudas. In the same period, Theudas offered to divide the river Jordan, and to lead his four hundred followers across on dry land, as a proof of his Messianic power ; but the Roman Fadus, with a troop of cavalry, intercepted them on the banks of the river and beheaded their leader.

Bar-Kochba, as we have seen (130–134 A.D.), was accepted by the best scholar of his day as the Messiah, organised the Jews of the Dispersion to revolt against Rome, captured Jerusalem, lost it, and was finally vanquished with enormous losses.

Serenus. About the year 720 A.D. a Syrian, Serenus, appeared as Messiah, offered to release the Jews from Talmudical regulations, to lead them back to Palestine, and to expel the Moslems. After considerable disturbance Serenus was captured and brought before the Khalif Yezid, who handed him over to his co-religionists for punishment.

Abu-Isa. About 750 A.D., Abu-Isa of Ispahan announced that he was the last of five forerunners of the Messiah, and gathered 10,000 Jews to fight for freedom from the yoke of foreign rulers. He proclaimed the abrogation of sacrificial worship, forbade the use of wine and meat, and prescribed prayer seven times a day. After some success, Abu-Isa was killed in battle; but his sect of Ispahanites persisted for several centuries.

David Al-Roy. About 1160 A.D., David Al-Roy, or Ibn Alruchi, gathered a force of warlike Jews from Azerbaijan and announced to the Jews of Asia that he was appointed by God to deliver them from the yoke of the Moslems and to lead them back to Palestine. At his command the Jews of Bagdad sat on their roofs in green robes on the appointed night awaiting deliverance; but the enterprise failed, and David Al-Roy was given over to death by his own father-in-law.

A Messiah in Yemen. About 1172, in Yemen, Arabia, a Jewish enthusiast called himself the forerunner of the Messiah, persuaded his adherents to have a community of goods, and caused civil commotion. A wise letter from Maimonides warned the Yemen Jews, that " it is wrong to calculate the Messianic period, as the Yemen enthusiast thinks he has succeeded in doing; for it can never be exactly determined, it having been purposely concealed by the prophets as a deep secret."

Sabbataï Zebi. The notorious career of Sabbataï Zebi (1626–1676) was inspired by the mystical speculations of the Kabbala, which pointed to the year of the world 5408 (= 1648 A.D.) as the era of redemption. A prophecy was produced, testifying of this Sabbataï : " He shall quell the great Dragon : he is the true Messiah, and shall wage war without weapons." From Smyrna to Egypt, Salonika, and Constantinople, Sabbataï made triumphal processions, and was received with enthusiasm. Distant communities sent ambassadors with gifts. The Sultan interviewed the Messiah and said, if he were divine, the arrows of his soldiers could do no harm. Sabbataï then renounced his claims and became a Moslem. His adherents did not desert him, but maintained that his purpose was to convert Islam. He died in peace, and a remnant of his sect still persists. By this movement, says a Jewish historian, " Judaism was covered with shame . . . its followers everywhere in the East and in the West, with exceptions, became slaves to a delusion which made them the ridicule of the world."

Jewish intellect misdirected. From such instances it appears that the Jewish intellect often found the Talmud a heavy burden, grievous to be borne, and that, like other faiths, it created for itself a realm of mysticism. It is also clear that when secular subjects were studied, greater success was attained by Jewish scholars in that field than in the real understanding of the Penta-teuch. The list of false Messianic movements, the readiness to accept a counterfeit for the real, is a striking commentary on what is written : " Many shall come, saying, I am the Christ ; and shall lead many astray " (Matt. 24⁵).

Restoration of Palestine to Jews. An important element in Judaism, which is still of general interest, is the relation of the Jewish religion to its ancient habitation in Palestine. Is Judaism a religion ? If so, does it require a national home ? or is it a society, seeking for national indepen-dence and territorial sovereignty? The answer to these questions involves the nature of religion, the constitution of nations, and the principles of international equity.

What claim has any nation to a home ? If we could ask primitive peoples at the dawn of history what right they had to their territories, they would answer as we do :

> " Our fathers' sepulchres are here,
> And here our children dwell."

Possession is and was a primary and valid argu-ment against dispossession. Was any change permissible in the occupation of territory ? Can any race maintain that its land to-day must be for ever kept safe for its posterity alone ? The practice of mankind has generally conformed to the maxim that " He may take who has the power, and he may keep who can." National cohesion made boundaries more rigid and definite, and tended to restrict hospitality to strangers. Yet the early nations were not insensible to the claims of mercy and humanity. When drought had brought famine on Canaan, Egypt again and again shared the produce of the Nile with starving refugees from the desert. Migrations for food and pasture were frequent, and excited no hostility among nomads. A settler, of course, accepted the religion of the new country, as Ruth did when she settled in Bethlehem. The Jewish philosopher Spinoza, speaking for his own generation, 1630–1697, confirms that ancient usage, and holds that citizens have no right on rational grounds to resist the recognised religion of the State. Among the Greeks and Romans, religion was also closely connected with territory. Religion was not the affair of the individual, but was prescribed, official, an organised cult. " The god must be officially recognised by the State, and his ceremonial must be the one prescribed by the official experts of the State. Other gods, and therefore their ceremonials, are heterodox, and, like magic, are forbidden." The Pilgrim Fathers in the *Mayflower* renounced their homes in order to preserve the freedom of their religion ;

they were fortunate in finding a spacious land with few people and no religious scruples. Had America been full of Pharisees enforcing the precepts of Shammai, the pilgrims, as avowed Nonconformists, could not have been permitted to land.

The world in general had thus made some rules on the reception of strangers and the recognition of religion, when Judaism lost Jerusalem. The Jews themselves looked on their banishment as a punishment for sin, and their hope was that after expiation and penitence a Messiah would restore them, as they had been restored from Chaldæa. What is the real teaching of the Bible on the possession of Palestine as an essential in Hebrew religion ?

The Bible and the land. There is in the Bible a growth of opinion, a variety of reflections on Hebrew claims to the Holy Land. The Song of Deborah makes no apology for winning the battle against Sisera, and enjoying the spoils of victory (Judg. 5). The tribe of Dan, desiring more room, ascertained from their spies that the men of Laish were dwelling quiet and careless ; and they smote them with the edge of the sword and settled down in the district they had conquered (Judg. 18). By the sword, Israel had won its victory over the Amorites ;

and by the sword, Saul and David extended their sovereign independence. Conquest is then thought to be a sufficient reason for annexation. It was the prophet Amos who first began to inquire by what moral title-deeds Israel might hope to remain in Palestine. " The eyes of the Lord God are upon the sinful kingdom, and I will destroy it from off the face of the earth " (Amos 9⁸). Palestine was not to be made a safe place for Israel, if Israel became morally unworthy.

Moral claims to territory. The disciples of the prophets began to find victory in war insufficient as a claim to their home. The iniquity of the Amorite, they said, deserved to be suppressed ; so, looking backward, they postulated a war of extermination by Divine command. The editors of Deuteronomy represent Israel as the lineal heir of Abraham, who had hallowed the land by his presence. Another thinker excludes the Edomites because their ancestor, Esau, though the elder son, had sold his birthright to Jacob, the ancestor of Israel. The Priests' Code, which became the Magna Charta of Pharisaism, fixed the Hebrew religion more firmly to the soil of Palestine. It has no hesitation in sanctioning war for defence, and authorises the priest to accompany the army. As a model for the future, a typical war with Midian is described in detail in Numbers, ch. 31. It is cruel reading, but there is no need to believe it to be actual history. It is as if we in Scotland described an imaginary encounter between Scots and Picts, and allowed the victor to give a model chastisement to the offender. Twelve thousand Hebrew soldiers, without the loss of a single life, exterminate the men of Midian ; and carry back to Moses, women, children, and countless cattle. Moses is represented as reproving the mercy of the soldiers in sparing so many : he orders them to kill all the boys and their mothers, sparing only the unmarried girls, of whom there are 32,000. And this narrative becomes in the Law a celestial imperative. A Jew, said Josephus, would sooner forfeit his life than change a syllable of the Torah. Conquest, if commanded by the Law, would seem sufficient to the Priests' Code for much more than annexation. But there is a more intimate association of the individual with the land. The primary obligation of Judaism is circumcision, and its institution is traced to Abraham and to the promise of Canaan for his posterity (Gen. 17). An incidental right is elaborated by the Priests' Code in describing how Abraham insisted on paying the full price, " current money with the merchant," for the cave of Machpelah, when he bought it from the

Hittites.   There three generations were buried ; and this continuity gave a certain ancestral right to the country.   The supreme claim advanced by the Priests' Code arises from his doctrine of Creation.   Time and lands, law and divine right began all together ; the Creator is the Proprietor of the Universe, and His will is intimated to mankind through the Priests' Code.

Religion transcends geography.   It may be held that these are antiquated exaggerations of theoretical zeal ; but so far as Judaism maintains the Divine Authority and perpetual validity of every part of the Mosaic Law, these principles must be treated as still living.   The world is familiar with the evangelic religion, which rejected the Priests' Code and revived the universal aims of the great prophets.   But Judaism still looked for a Messiah and longed for restoration.   The prophetic and evangelical religion found a home in any land ; it did not depend on the Temple, or the Holy City, or the ordained sacrifices.   The field was the world ; and the apostles went forth willingly to be a light to lighten the Gentiles. The gnawing nostalgia of the Hebrew exiles has never been felt by their compatriots who preached the Gospel.   The prophets taught that a man should take his religion with him wherever he went.   True religion does not depend on geography, any more than do philosophy or music or mathematics. It is by admitting this view that citizenship has been granted to Jews in the lands of their dispersion. By claiming a national home for their religion, they are doing what no other religion would be allowed by general consent to contemplate. Suppose they were granted a homogeneous state, what would be the position of any one who sought to settle among them ? If the Law were rigidly enforced with revived sacrifices and rabbinical regulations, no tourist could be admitted till he had accepted at least the seven precepts applicable to all the descendants of Noah. The Jewish deputies to Napoleon's Sanhedrim were asked whether they considered Frenchmen as their brethren ; and they replied in the affirmative, quoting the command to " love thy neighbour as thyself " (Lev. 19$^{33\text{-}35}$). In this answer they widened the scope of Talmudic regulations. So long as Israel was under foreign rule, it was prudent to be civil to Gentiles. But even so great a figure as Maimonides does not hesitate to say : " But when the hand of Israel is strong upon them (the idolators), we are forbidden to suffer an idolator amongst us, even so much as to sojourn incidentally, or to pass from place to place with merchandise " (*Old Paths*, McCaul, pp. 39,

40). The Thirteen Principles of the Jewish Faith, formulated by Maimonides, testify in Article 12 : " I believe with perfect faith in the coming of the Messiah, and, though he tarry, I will wait daily for his coming." Acknowledging obligations so complicated, the restored community in Palestine would not be able to offer to strangers the same hospitality which they receive in foreign countries. From the inherent nature of the religion to be provided with a territorial home, it does not appear that its character conforms to modern conceptions of spiritual religion. No other religion makes a similar claim, and the consensus of mankind would agree in rejecting a demand for territory in the name of religion.

International custom. How does the usage of international intercourse bear on this proposal, apart from religious considerations ? If one " national " visit the country of another, he makes courteous request for a passport ; and he carefully conforms to the regulations of the land he visits. If he be a missionary, offering to bestow gifts of healing and teaching, he must first submit his principles to examination, and promise obedience to the laws of his host. There is no nation which expects its members to claim equal rights in foreign nations and also to retain their citizenship in an exclusive realm of their own. Any man who demands to become a shareholder in any company without price or purchase, would be considered eccentric in financial circles. Yet this is the position into which the Zionist proposal would bring all men and women of Jewish birth who are citizens in their present homes. They ask the world to receive members of a race which separates itself from the rest of humanity by its dogmas, into equal rights and " equal economic opportunity " in any nation where they may desire to settle. And this the world as a whole has become willing to grant them. But they also ask the world to reverse the course of history and to reinstate them in a national home, where others already have a national home. However warmly the world may sympathise with the sufferings of wandering Israel, it can hardly bid defiance to the universal axioms of international justice.

Justice or generosity? It would be a new and a noble thing on earth if civilised humanity took counsel together, striving to do an act of generosity beyond the sphere of strict justice. " If thine enemy hunger, give him food," was considered an idle paradox ; yet after the recent War the maxim was practised on a vast international scale. Nations are governed by their interests ; and, even with individuals, any departure from equal justice is apt to make compassion disastrous in the end. Homer and Plato were probably the most powerful agents in restoring the independence of the Greeks a century ago ; and it may be pleaded that Abraham and Isaiah deserve equal regard. The self-determination of small nations has been a favourite theme with non-combatant orators during the late War. Never before were there so many kindly souls on earth ready to welcome a picturesque illustration of millennial romance. The horror of cruelty and the satisfaction of righting wrongs is happily very real to millions. Were Palestine empty, as devastated France was empty, no claimant could compete for universal sympathy with wandering Israel. But others, who are equally children of Abraham, who, unlike the ancient Amorite, share the winsome virtues of the Father of the Faithful, others already have their national home in Palestine. They have proved their title by centuries of possession, and they too have tender associations with the soil. All that can be wisely offered to Judaism in Palestine is a spiritual home, such as has contented other great communions for centuries. This would suffice to make Jerusalem the abode of peace, a centre of conciliation for all the great religions, a home of prayer for all the nations.

LECTURE IV.

CHRISTIANITY.

The Gospel and the silent past. THE earth had hundreds of forgotten races as its tenants two thousand years ago. It is well that they remained dumb and inarticulate, for the best they had to say would seem but crude and curious now. Their lot needs from us neither pity nor envy; too much misery or too happy innocence would be wrongly imputed to the anonymous races of the past. The same impartial Sun, whose light is sweet to us, made every child of nature glad: the same seasons offered the kindly fruits of the field to the whole human family, wheresoever they made their home. The whole race was loyal to the life they had, and bravely eager to welcome the life that was to be. If some groups showed more skill and power than others, it was because responsive souls were encouraged by obeying the potencies around them. These rare souls perceived the way of life more clearly, and taught their kinsmen how to profit by their insight.

By obedience and vision such a clan grew strong and multiplied; while those who were dull and disobedient remained stationary, or grew weaker than their neighbours. Even if it were true that the human infant of to-day is an epitome of all the brutalities that have been since organic life began, it must also be the heir of all the beauty that has blossomed in flowers, of all the merriment that finds place in young animals, of all the aspirations that have enobled the human soul. Our physical and spiritual inheritance has been compounded of the happy as well as the painful elements of life. The short span of recorded history has probably a darker proportion of mortal sin than the forgotten æons of the past. Our aboriginal forefathers were never uncared for, any more than the fowls of the air or the lilies of the field. The Eternal Father has never been indifferent to anything which He has made, although men did not know His name or acknowledge His existence.

Race reform. With what sort of human material had the Christian religion to deal when it appeared? At the beginning of the Christian era Australia was almost uninhabited, New Zealand empty, the Americas not without men who could build and even write, but who failed to advance or survive; India sadly meditating how to escape the vanity of life ; China diligent, prosaic, tenacious. No man knew where the seas ended, or where the heavens met the earth at the boundary of light and darkness. The coast-lands of the Mediterranean were the single centre of human knowledge and aspiration. Africa, Asia, and Europe were in contact around their central sea, and their best races had learned to appreciate one another. They had made some progress in the art and science of social life ; cities had become empires ; Rome had succeeded in subordinating a variety of races to the govern-ance of her system of law.

By force of arms ? In what form could a benefactor of the race offer genuine assistance at such a time ? Many peoples were still primitive, dominated by instinct and the senses, indifferent to past and future, disinclined to think deeply about themselves or their neighbours. Others at a higher stage were amusing themselves with imagination, mingling phantasy with experience, building up languages and mythology to the best of their ability. Only in Greece, Rome, and Israel had creative thought made real achieve-ments in the realm of the spirit. The chief good was differently conceived by each ; but the com-mand of men was the prize they all desired, and victory in war was considered to be the one

obvious way to world sovereignty.   The best of
Roman poets, choosing the noblest destiny he can
conceive for his country, thus defines her mission :

" Thine, O Roman, remember, to rule over every race !
    These be thine arts, thy glories, the ways of peace to
        proclaim,
    Mercy to show to the fallen, the proud with battle to tame."

And Judæa also, though forewarnèd, elected to
follow a similar ambition.

By increase   When such a temperament prevailed
of power ? among enlightened nations, would it
have been any boon to reveal the forces which
drive modern machinery ?   Would it be a blessing
to multiply the population of the earth, tenfold,
to its present numbers ? to provide them with
a universal language, and further their common
purpose ?   Union is strength—for good, but not
less for evil.   The confusion of tongues at Babel,
according to the old story, was meant to frustrate
an evil ambition of united men.   The barrier
of language began to fall away at Pentecost
because a pure intention pervaded the fellowship.
The best blessing it was possible to confer was to
cleanse the souls of individuals, to make the
character of the unit sound and good.   Then
increased numbers and increased capacity for
discovery would diffuse better national ambitions,
and would divert beneficent energy not to the con-

quest, but to the assistance of the less enlightened families of mankind. In viewing history as a whole, in trying to estimate various possibilities, it is not easy to see how a greater benefit could be conferred than by calling the Mediterranean races to work out their own salvation, and to raise the moral standard of the individual human life.

Or by activity of spirit ? To create an entirely new religion is not possible any more than to create an entirely new language. A thousand peoples have made their own languages which express similar thoughts and feelings, and the creative spirit is the same for all. There are hundreds of names for the " Sun," for " father," for " life," for " death " ; but all the different sounds that are used by diverse races describe the same realities. So the spirit of religion has influenced every race, and has moulded their customs and laws, their family life, their attitude to past and present. The soul of every people has its own history, and that history cannot be suddenly exchanged for the spiritual creations of another race. China and America could not exchange either their languages or their religions. What they have in common is a creative power which enables them to make words and to devise a means of expressing their religious traditions. Interchange of vocabulary or habits would be difficult and futile ; a new religion, which would conciliate diverse races, must appeal to the creative spirit common to all, must endeavour to awake that spirit into fresh activity and to bring it into living touch with the living God.

Greece indifferent, Rome agnostic, Jerusalem fortified against Gentiles. A universal religion could not be built on the foundation of Greek philosophy. True philosophy did succeed in creating noble characters, as in Socrates ; but its influence on the morals of the average man was negligible. It did not profess to speak with Divine authority, and had no concern about saving that which was lost. Romans like Cicero and Julius Cæsar were only vaguely groping after a plausible doctrine of Divine Providence ; a common feeling in Rome was that, in such speculations, there was nothing new and nothing true, and it did not matter. The one community on earth which had attained to definite convictions about religion, which had tested its doctrines by seven centuries of prosperity and adversity, which had applied the loftiest thought to the humblest member of its fellowship, was to be found among the Hebrews in Judæa and her colonies. Never perhaps on earth was there a race so permeated by a definite theistic belief, so rigidly regulated in personal and communal practice, so free on the whole from the grosser sensual vices, so thoroughly clear about duty, and so loyally eager to fulfil it. It was not an easy thing for Greek, Roman, or Judæan to exceed the righteousness of the scribes and Pharisees, and to enter into a higher realm of religious life. This was the task which Christianity undertook, and its appearance marks the point when Hebrew religion diverged into two distinct forms, Judaism and Christianity.

Prophetic obedience to the Spirit and Pharisaic obedience to the Law. The common foundation of both these faiths was laid by the prophets Amos, Hosea, and their successors. They had made it clear that the Deity is a moral Person making moral demands on mankind, and intent on securing universal welfare. The prophets knew that they had the direct inspiration of God, and the reasonableness of their teaching was only a secondary justification in their feeling. Their contemporaries did not claim to be inspired, but they could appreciate inspiration in others; just as many can study and enjoy great poetry though they are not poets themselves. Inspiration does not come in answer to human desire; and the voice of prophecy had ceased with Malachi (450 B.C.). The influence of the vanished prophets impelled their disciples to collect their words, to revise their Laws, and finally to establish the Five Books of Mosaic Law as the constitution of the Hebrew fellowship. The Law soon became so powerful that prophecy was considered dangerous. If any man arose professing to be a prophet, he was to be thrust through by his own father and mother (Zech. 13$^{3-6}$). Contact with Greek thought had caused grave danger, and the victory of the Maccabees hardened the hostility against the heathen world. A hedge of minor regulations was devised to protect the Jew against possible infringement of the regulations of the Pentateuch. All the words of the Torah were considered to be of equal authority, and to require equal recognition, equal obedience. The duty of a Pharisee comprised no less than 613 divine commands, 248 positive, 365 negative. Regulations for Temple service, civil life, and agriculture in Palestine could not be observed in foreign countries ; but for the Israelite abroad there still remained 369 binding commands, 126 positive, and 243 negative, not to mention Rabbinic additions. The chief end of Creation was to furnish a sphere for the observance of the Law ; the Law was divine, eternal, of perpetual validity, not to be tampered with by man. " He who asserts that the Torah is not from Heaven, has no part in the world to come." " He who says that Moses wrote even one verse of his own knowledge, is a denier and a despiser of the Word of God." The desire of the Hebrews to convert the Gentiles had been destroyed by the painful conflicts for national independence. The penalty of death was intimated in the Temple to any Gentile who intruded into the sacred area. The mere suspicion that St. Paul had brought an Ephesian within the holy precincts was enough to cause a dangerous riot (Acts 21²⁷ᶠ·). " The man who would go up to the hill of Jehovah must be one who has not eaten shell-fish or pork, nor opened his shop on Sabbath, nor touched a dead body, nor used a spoon, handed to him by a Gentile, without washing it." This fastidious care was a reaction from bitter experience at the hands of the Gentiles. Judaism, in the interests of self-preservation, had to defend itself against all contamination from outside influences ; but in doing so it had made the universal morality of the prophets more difficult of attainment. Any critic of the dominant system expressed himself at his peril ; the only possible prophet was Elijah as herald of the Messiah, who, far from criticising the Law, was to impose it on the whole Gentile world.

Hope of prophetic revival. The religion of the Spirit, though thus severely controlled by the Pharisaic system, was kept alive by the Psalms and the growth of conscience. Inspired prophets or poets do not appear at the command of mortal men. Many nations have never had a great poet ; some have one, others several, none have very many ; and no race has been able to produce an unbroken succession of great poets. So, in the sphere of the higher religions, the spiritual inheritance of a social group has to be fused into organic beauty by a single soul before it can command the devotion of posterity. When such a spirit appears, his influence travels beyond his own race and language, and is welcomed by strangers far away. Though prophets ceased in Israel, the hope of their reappearance never vanished. God is a Spirit, and men are living spirits ; is the communion of Spirit with spirit restricted to one race, to one language, to one generation in the heroic past ? Even Philo thought that the wisdom of Greece must have been secretly borrowed from Moses ; but the prophetic temper in the story of Jonah maintains that cruel Nineveh is the object of the Divine mercy. The revival of prophecy, the gift of the Holy Spirit, was the ardent desire of the company of the Essenes. By ascetic observances, by the free exercise of personal prayer, by community of goods (" All mine is thine " was the maxim of the settlement), by personal cleanliness, and daily baths, this brotherhood of some four

Essenes.

thousand members, segregated on the coast of the Dead Sea, had led a devout life for two or three generations before the Christian era ; and the express purpose of their withdrawal from ordinary intercourse was that they might bring again the direct communion of God with men. Josephus the historian made trial of their life and discipline for several years before attaching himself to the Pharisees. John the Baptist may have had some connection with them before he began to preach the necessity for reformation. Centuries later, in the Talmudic schools of Babylon, it was said in praise of Anan ben David, son of the Exilarch Solomon (761 A.D.) : " If he had lived at the time when the Temple was still standing, he would have been vouchsafed the gift of prophecy." Hence the aspiration of devout individuals as well as the rigid observance of the Law centred on the hope of re-establishing the living communion of God with man and the diffusion of righteousness over the whole world.

The Author of the new faith. The Christianity which prevailed against the wit and wealth, the learning and martial power of the Roman Empire, did not come into being without an efficient Creator. In looking at Christianity as one of the Semitic religions, it is not possible to explain to those of other faiths all that the disciples of Christ acknowledge in His personality.   What can be done is to estimate the effects of His work on the history of mankind.   Though the form of some of His utterances may find parallels in older books, though there were pre-existing materials of human thought, language, and custom, the creative spirit which called the new faith into being was His alone.   The axioms of geometry have a validity which is independent of the character of Euclid ;   but Christianity cannot be severed from the Personality of Christ.   His teaching would have had no effect if His words had been spoken by Herod or Pontius Pilate, by Shammai or Caiaphas ;   for the lives of these men were such as to falsify the evangelic temperament.   He wrote no book ;   He appealed neither to visions nor to the message of an angel.   In His own Name and by the unique authority of His own Personality He created the Church.

Universal scope.   The evangelic religion appeals to motives which are independent of race, language, nationality, occupation, sex, or climate ; that is, the appeal is not to the accidents that divide mankind, but to the spiritual capacities which belong to all.   It calls into life the creative spirit which made languages, used thought, generated varieties of religion.   A new humanity was being called into life, " after the image of

him that created it ; where there cannot be
Greek and Jew, circumcision and uncircumcision,
barbarian, Scythian, bondman, freeman : but
Christ is all, and in all " (Col. 3[11]). True religion
consists not in careful dietary regulations, nor in
abstinence from wine—" neither in meat nor
drink, but in righteousness and peace and joy in
the Holy Ghost " (Rom. 14[17]). Such a religion
should not be called Semitic, but humanist; just
as the imputation of nationality to the Deity is
an impossible anthropomorphism.

The rule of God. It was not easy to find a name for
this new faith. It was sometimes
called " the kingdom of heaven." For contemporary Jews this phrase meant that they
should escape from Roman sovereignty and be
free to obey the rule of God with no human
interference. The Gospel had to use the name,
but had to replace the current associations by
an entirely new conception. If a man has felt
in his soul the power of the Divine Spirit, such a
man is said to have been baptized with fire, to be
born again. If his contact with the Holy Spirit
has been genuine, his deepest impulse is to reverence and obey the Voice he has heard. Isaiah
had had such a new birth during the solemn
service of the Temple : Amos had heard the
Divine Voice in the wilderness ; Ezekiel tells

how it came to him. In all these cases the first effect was to make the prophet conscious of his unworthiness to be in the Divine Presence. The same humility and sense of sin is awakened in Peter and Paul. In the life of Christ there is no sign of any break with past experience; inspiration with Him is not intermittent, varying in intensity and assurance, excited by great occasions and then dormant. The whole life is pervaded by the same sure confidence in fulfilling the work assigned by the Father. St. Luke's record of the sense of purpose in the later boyhood of Christ (Luke 2⁴⁹) is confirmed by another consideration. Jeremiah was almost singular in Hebrew history in renouncing marriage. General custom in the apostolic age required early marriages. But such a possibility for Christ is never contemplated in the Gospels. He knew He was different from other men and had a different work to do. There is no trace of trial and error in the creation of the Church; three years allowed no time for tentative experiments. Human nature and its sense of Deity are the soil in which the seed is to be sowed. The Roman soldier, the busy Greek, the Syro-Phœnician, the Samaritan, the priest, the Levite, the publican, the fisherman, the day-labourer, the blind beggar, Cæsar himself—all have their claim as human beings; all are children of the

Heavenly Father and worthy of receiving life more abundantly.

Use of the Old Testament. Hence arose Christ's confidence in measuring afresh the value of the Scriptures. The narrative of the Evangelists concerning Christ's deeds makes frequent allusions to the Old Testament; but His own words are conspicuously independent of proof texts. To criticise the Law meant to claim superiority over Moses, and only Divine Authority could, according to the Pharisees, make any change in the Law. The Epistle to the Hebrews admits this presupposition, and makes an elaborate defence of the abolition of sacrificial worship, showing that Christ's sanction had the necessary vindication. To change the customs of the Law was treason to the Pharisaic faith; and the fact that Saul stood by, consenting to the stoning of Stephen, shows how the best of Pharisees were ready to let this Law run its course. The Pauline Epistles acknowledge the Divine Law with deeper deference than do the Gospels. Christ merely gives prominence to the essence of the Law and the Prophets by selecting the Fatherhood of God and the Brotherhood of man as the chief end of religion. He uses the words of Prophets and Psalmists to confirm the experience of His own disciples. The One Righteous God, who requires righteousness from mankind, is the same Heavenly Father who is not content with inflicting the penalty of transgression, but who loves mankind even in their sin and sends forth His Spirit to deliver them from misery and to rescue them from failure. The Spirit that spoke to Isaiah was ready to speak to the souls of living men in every age. The Spirit which taught the prophets that God was just, that He abhorred cruelty, that He delighted in mercy, was seen by the disciples to direct every word and deed in the life of Christ Himself. Hence the disciples gradually learned to feel the guidance of the Holy Spirit, to wait obediently for inspiration, to acquire an intuitive perception of the right thing to say or do, to know when they were following the devices and desires of their own hearts instead of speaking " in the Spirit."

Personal obedience to the Holy Spirit. The new faith is first of all a new personal experience, a sense of sin forgiven, of living guidance, of hope and peace. By obedience the convert grows to a clearer perception of the will of God. The gift of the Spirit can be conveyed from one who has it to one who has not yet felt it. Giver and receiver of this new life increase each other's happiness, and together they are eager to bless others with their baptism of fire. No two human beings are exactly alike, but all who are recipients of the evangelic grace are ready to say that " man's chief end is to glorify God and to enjoy Him for ever." The desire of the true convert is always that the whole family of mankind should share the happiness which he feels. God is ruling his spirit; the " kingdom of heaven " has come and is present with him. This kingdom is not relegated to a future world, but is here present in the souls that are ready to receive it. The company of disciples, as time went on, were sometimes looked upon as a new kingdom. " Thy kingdom come " means nearly the same as the following petition : " Thy will be done in earth, as it is in heaven."

The service of the Messiah. What then did the world need ? and what did Christ desire it to receive ? The desires of the nations were as the Milky Way, innumerable, incomprehensible, inaccessible. It would be a strange world where every one got all they wanted. Those who had attained their highest hopes were generally disappointed. National ambitions were such that victory for one meant harsh servitude for another. Men as a whole must be born again ; they must live through a childhood in communion with the Holy Spirit, and grow to a better manhood and efficiency, learning to do justly, to love mercy, and to walk humbly with God. Their desires were to be so directed that the good of one man should never bring any harm to his neighbour. Peace on earth and goodwill among men was the best boon that could be given ; and the true glory of Israel was not self-preservation, but to be a light to lighten the Gentiles. Such was the end, clearly foreseen from first to last with all it must involve for Himself, which Christ accepted as the Messianic purpose of His Heavenly Father. " The cup which my Father hath given me, shall I not drink it ? "

Parable made hearers use their own minds. How was this great task to be accomplished ? The time was short, and men had many misconceptions. The use of popular language was apt to encourage dangerous illusions. He would not call Himself Messiah, but allowed the title " Son of Man," which helped to cancel nationality. To avoid phrases which had lost their meaning He taught in parables. His choice of this form betokens His mastery of a clear purpose, the ability to detach Himself from current controversies and to reawaken fresh thinking. The parable was not beyond the capacity of His hearers ; it invested familiar experience with beauty, as in a picture : the picture was significant with meaning which the disciple had to discover for himself.

The dawning perception of the disciple was delighted in realising the meaning; and the simplicity and beauty of form made it impossible to forget the spiritual truth which the parable had been devised to convey.

"Lambs among wolves." The training of the Apostles was much more intimate and continuous than the instruction through parables. The kind of men Christ chose for carrying out His beneficent purpose is another proof of originality. When war is declared, who will select the one in a myriad who may receive the Victoria Cross? Nicodemus, Gamaliel, the rich young ruler, the type of Josephus, were unequal through their earthly associations to the work of Apostles. By the nature of their calling, fishermen are trained in the school of experience to be patient and persevering; they must never use force or violence, must never be disappointed by failure, and must remain adventurous to the last. Of such were the first disciples, Andrew and Peter, James and John. By neighbourly friendship, by their response to the preaching of John the Baptist, these men had become acquainted with Jesus; and when they received His call to leave their usual work and to follow Him, they did not hesitate. The prospects of their new career were not concealed. They would never acquire lands or houses or money. They were very gravely warned against the desire for money. "Ye cannot serve God and mammon"; you cannot be a missionary and a millionaire—one or other perhaps, but never both. The moral censure of a millionaire is negligible; the control of Samaria's finance would close men's hearts against any spiritual gifts they had to offer; such control would only win men like Simon Magus. The labourer is worthy of his maintenance; and if you are true to the Holy Spirit, your message will always find responsive hearts who will be eager to supply the little you require for yourselves. The herald of good tidings, filled with benevolence, might expect a welcome everywhere; but that will not be your fate. Men shall say all manner of evil against you falsely, for My sake; but you must never return hatred for persecution. God desires to redeem the souls of persecutors and to make them just and gentle; you must be perfect as your Father in heaven is perfect; and, against nature, you must love your enemies, and pray for them that despitefully use you. But ye will receive power from on high; and the purpose of God shall prosper in your hands. "Behold, I send you forth as lambs among wolves."

Very gradually He disclosed to them how His own mission was to end. Not in word only but in very deed, He taught them to obey the Holy Spirit even unto death. The chief end of *The fruits of the Spirit are the mark of a true Church.* a Christian is not to be crucified ; but if testimony to Divine Truth involves death, the disciples must be prepared to face martyrdom. When penitence has been kindled in the heart of humanity, martyrdom will become obsolete. Though their eyes should see Him no more, they would not be left alone. Through the Holy Spirit, God would make Christ's presence more real to His disciples than it had been during the days of His flesh. They would be able to convey the gift of Divine grace to strangers, and the Gospel would be preached in the whole wide world. A new fellowship would be created on earth, including all races and languages. The mark of the Christian society would be its dependence on the Holy Spirit, and its power to produce the fruits of the Spirit. No outward form is prescribed for the Church that is to be. Some Christians may cultivate the expectant attitude that waits for the Spirit and trusts no external form ; others may train themselves to receive Divine grace through the Sacraments of repentance and communion ; others again may find in study, in the discipline of intellect, emotion, and will, the corroboration of the Divine life of which they have been made partakers. Brave men in all lands and times have been able to improvise an organisation for their armies ; the essential thing is that they should have courage. So Christians, having the guidance of the Holy Spirit, will be able to devise forms for expressing their common worship. Each race and nation may hallow the dealing of Divine Providence with their forefathers and blend their own particular heritage with the universal adoration of Christendom. " He that hath an ear, let him hear what the Spirit saith unto the churches."

Fishers of men.   To have in three years inspired a hundred souls to give fitful and faltering obedience to the Spirit of God, would seem but a slender basis for a new religion. But though there were few Christians when Christ was crucified, their faith was true and real. To be false to the new Spirit was worse than death, as Judas Iscariot decided. To be loyal, meant to acquire a superhuman courage. The new power which had come into their souls gave them easy control of the blind carnal appetites which ruled the mass of men. The spiritual purpose displaced the attraction of bodily pleasures for them. If a man cannot master his own body, he will never be able to give much help to his neighbours. The first effect of the Christian life was to add

self-governance to faith. But the happy health-
fulness of a few selected souls did not fulfil their
Master's command. Any pure and noble life
shines like a light, and is a boon to all spectators.
But passive philanthropy fell far short of the
evangelic obligation. The ancient prophets had
said that the Servant of JHVH must make
Damascus and Egypt, Babylon and Persia,
conscious that the Judge of all the earth abhors
cruelty and will punish unrighteousness. Had
these great Powers been obedient to a Righteous
God, small nations would have had nothing to
fear. The Gospel acknowledges the same Divine
obligation to convert the earthly sovereignties ; the
world must become just and gentle, else mortal men
were better dead. " Go ye therefore and teach
all nations " was the ideal of the prophets ; and
the few disciples of Christ felt its urgency as
none had ever done before.

Emigration for new motives. For the first time in history there
appeared an order of travellers, in-
different to trade or sight-seeing, intent
only on kindling the holy fire which had brought
happiness and health to their own souls. Judaism,
said one of its apologists, was no more a proselytising body than the British House of Lords. " The
average Jew," says the noblest of his exponents,
" of even 50 to 80 A.D., was not continually

worrying about the future of the Gentile world, or about the duties of proselytising" (*Beginnings of Christianity*, Part I., Jackson and Lake, p. 36. Macmillan, 1920). The ardour of the ancient prophets had to wait for the Apostles to translate it into reality. The patriotic love of Jerusalem became a passion to make the whole earth a Holy Land. The migrating evangelists had much to endure ; and they were commanded to overcome evil with good, never to return hatred for injustice. When this temperament had time to make itself felt, the missionaries ceased to be regarded as undesirable aliens. They were welcomed as benefactors of the lands they had evangelised. They had not come seeking their own good at the expense of their hosts ; they had come to offer the best they had for nothing in return. They had no reward for themselves in prospect ; yet what finer homage could these first missionaries receive than the reverent honour offered by Scotland to St. Andrew, by London to St. Paul, by Rome to St. Peter ? The Galilean fishermen had been faithful to Him who sent them forth ; they knew through the Spirit their immediate duty and they did it. Only the future could show how much was to be built on their fidelity and obedience. They were to have their place in " the household of God, being built upon the foundation of the apostles and prophets, Christ Jesus himself being the chief corner stone " (Eph. 2^{20}).

The company of Christians grew

The new society requires each man to bear his own burden. rapidly in numbers, and had soon to measure mutual obligations among themselves. The new benevolence could never allow a neighbour to die of want which could be relieved. To give bread alone would seem altogether insufficient; if spiritual peace were given and received, material help would follow inevitably. Hence for a time some had all things in common. Where benevolence reigned, natural indolence tempted some to allow others to carry their burden. The sanity of the faith decided that those who could carry their own burden should not allow themselves to become passive dependents of the community. "It is more blessed to give than to receive." "He who will not work, neither let him eat." The world cannot be maintained by general idleness; nor can religious zeal exempt any from doing their part of the world's work in procuring daily bread. It is not possible to be generous by proxy, to enter the house of Dives and to carry something handsome out for Lazarus; it must be at your own cost that you can be truly generous. He who provideth not for his own is an infidel and hath denied the faith. The obligations of parents cannot rightly be transferred to the Church. All these conformities to equal justice were enacted and enforced in a society whose glory was to show mercy and compassion even to those who had forfeited all claim to forbearance. The same axioms of self-reliance and parental responsibility are found by experience to be fundamental in secular social systems, which profess to be founded on justice and equality.

Benevolence is prescribed for the sick. But many are born in weakness; and some through sickness or disease cannot hope to earn for themselves as much as their infirmities make necessary. They must depend on others or cease to live. To minister to their needs without hurting their feelings was a new art, which the disciples learned from Christ. The man who had been born blind was not being punished for the sins of his parents, but was teaching all who had eyes to see to be thankful for their blessings and to use God's gifts in relieving suffering. The maimed and the halt and the blind could receive the Holy Spirit, and could kindle living compassion and win reverence from strong men, more successfully than those who had known no suffering. The Gospel thus conferred a high dignity on those who reached holiness through suffering; and it also generated a new enthusiasm for the relief of sickness and the cure of disease. Half the Gospel is concerned with works of healing; and by the fruits of its work the medical profession can claim evangelic ordination. The purer morality created by the Gospel would tend to remove the cause of much misery; spiritual force instantly healed many forms of distemper and dissipated many very real, though illusory, hallucinations. Each century has its own diagnosis of certain maladies; one century inflicts the death-penalty for witchcraft, while the next pronounces the offence impossible. When men fancied that their illness was due to some disastrous configuration of the stars or to some diabolic contrivance of ill-disposed neighbours, the remedies were either unthinkable or revengeful. The mere belief that sin could be forgiven, that guilt could be removed, that diseases could be healed, brought a fresh inspiration of hope; it encouraged every effort to cure the ills of the body as well as the sickness of the soul. It was a right response to the evangelic intention which made the early Bishops of the Church compete with each other in providing homes for strangers and hospitals for the sick. Basil of Cæsarea had an establishment where strangers were hospitably entertained, and medical attendance and nursing were provided for all kinds of sickness. The physicians resided within the walls ; and work-shops were provided for all the artisans and labourers whose services were needed. The Christian charity which created such institutions was a valuable element in communal life ; and it is the impulse in the Gospel that directed the energy of the Christian community towards such works of beneficence.

Immortality in theory. The Gospel offers men Divine Grace, and bids them work for the healing of the nations. It also brought to man's soul a new assurance of immortality. It has caused surprise that the Mosaic Law makes no demand on a future life as a sanction for the Decalogue. Before the composition of the Mosaic books was understood, it was suggested that Moses had seen the cult of the Dead carried to excess in Egypt, and had therefore excluded the idea from his legislation. The best prophets were mainly concerned about defining the present duty of living men. It has recently been said that, about 350 B.C., " the average Jew believed that, so far as any bliss or happiness was concerned (whether higher or lower), death was the end : by 50 A.D. he believed that for the righteous, at any rate, the higher happiness would actually not be experienced till beyond the grave." In the book of Daniel it is said that some of those who had perished in the persecution would revive to receive reward or punishment after victory had been attained. The good often suffer in this life and the wicked often prosper. It became a common assumption that there must be a future life in which merit and demerit would be adjusted to their proper consequences. The Resurrection was matter of controversy between the Pharisees and Sadducees. At best it was a fond desire, a pleasing hope, not founded on the Divine authority of the Law.

Immortality in experience. Far different was the feeling of the first Christians. They had been made conscious of the living influence of the Holy Spirit. The sorrow of Good Friday was turned into joy by their experience of Easter Sunday morning. They knew by sure conviction that the Spirit of Christ had conquered the king of terrors ; they discovered that the human soul has a treasure far more precious than its lease of earthly human life. The gain of the whole world is mean and miserable in comparison with this treasure of the soul. Henceforward the Apostles are found to be radiant with hope and high intentions. They had on the first Easter morning acquired the conviction that Christ was alive, that His Spirit had been made victorious by their Heavenly Father. They began to live a new life in constant communion with the Holy Spirit. And though they lived so much under the power of the world to come, it is to them we owe the noblest definitions of the duty that is proper to the life that now is. They bade us work cheerfully in sure hope of a time when all cruelty shall cease, when all sin and disease shall disappear, when the whole earth will be glad, living in peace and hope. The task they prescribed for our present life was to establish peace and goodwill among men universally. The assurance of immortal life for the soul was one of the causes of the rapid diffusion of the new religion.

The Church in the Roman Empire. The evangelic ideal had been announced to a few honest spirits. Was it to remain a dream, shadowing forth another Utopia like that of Ezekiel or Plato? The opposition at the beginning seemed omnipotent. The parent faith of Judaism, instead of helping, exerted itself to stamp out the Galilean heresy. The Roman Empire with universal sovereignty took a long time to notice the difference between Judaism and Christianity, but continued to despise both. The best of the Roman emperors enacted the severest measures against these new nonconformists. Ten persecutions and the blood of many martyrs convinced the Romans that the Christians were not lacking in the virtues they respected most—courage and veracity. Investigation proved that Christians had good habits, pure homes, and a friendly disposition to all sorts and conditions of men. The conquest of the principalities and powers became possible, when strong men felt the constraint of honour and justice. No doubt the Gospel put restraint on the exercise of power. Alexander Stewart, the Wolf of Badenoch, felt the restriction of his liberty so acutely that he resolved to destroy all Christian scruples by burning the cathedral at Elgin. The building was burned ; but the scruples gathered fresh force and kindled penitence and some efforts to make amends. A morbid fancy has in modern times represented that men of exceptional power have been poisoned and enfeebled by retaining the remnants of a Christian conscience. Let the giants realise their own great ideas at any cost in meaner lives. One German colonel complained of his leader in the recent War that " he was instinctively an enemy of all manly strength of attack and battles for victory. He was far from understanding the German spirit. Perpetual compromises and negotiations—looking behind him all the time." The same kind of scruple in matters of religion is what, according to the critic of Christianity, has enfeebled European civilisation. History provides an experiment of strength in exercise with no religious scruples. Jenghiz Khan (1162–1227), the Mongol, had power and used it violently; and his career receives the abhorrence of succeeding generations. Christianity encourages the broken-hearted to hope, the oppressed to have patience, the offender to repent, the disciple to be active in doing good; and a noble part of Christian victory has been its success in persuading the strong to be just and gentle. In three hundred years the faith of the Prophets had through the Apostles become the official religion of the Roman Empire. Judaism had appealed to its Law and the Sword, and had failed; Christianity had appealed to the Spirit and the lives of its disciples, and had not failed. According to the story told of Julian, the last pagan emperor, it was indeed true that the Galilean had conquered. The conquest of the soul of Rome was a nobler achievement than victory over her arms.

LECTURE V.

THE MOSLEM RELIGION.

Arabia. ARABIA is the birthplace of Islam, the latest of the Semitic religions ; it appears also to have been the primeval nursery of all the sister races of what is called the " Semitic " family. This peculiar peninsula has divided its human progeny from all the rest of mankind ; its influence gives the " Semite " those distinctive marks which ancient fancy sought to explain by ascribing three sons to Noah. The area is four times the size of France, and the population something like that of Scotland. In all ages Arabia has been a shrine of the inorganic, unkindly to life. " A stack of plutonic rock, whereupon lie sandstones, and upon the sandstones limestones. There are, besides, great landbreadths of lavas and spent volcanoes "—such is the report of one who looked below the surface of Arabia. Fossils are rare, and represent " the remnants of a marine fauna which thrived over a considerable area during the Jurassic period." There is little wonder that the stone had a high place in the pantheon. Arabia has no Nile, and for lack of water millions of acres are lifeless. Wheat is scarce ; barley, if not required for the horses, affords a luxury for men. The camel for use, the horse for ornament, the date palm for food have been the best possessions of men. Part of the land was called " Happy," in contrast with the " Sandy " and the " Rocky " regions of the Peninsula. To live at all in " golden-aired " Arabia requires hereditary vigilance and tenacity ; to master Nature has hitherto proved too hard a task. Human skill made the land between the Tigris and Euphrates populous with great cities ; but man's ingenuity has made little impression on Arabia. Her sons have had to accept the natural conditions they could not change. Their motherland required to be clearly understood and carefully obeyed ; there is no mercy for either stupidity or indolence in the heart of the deserts. Strangers intrude at their peril ; and no conqueror has been able to settle. The sense of self-reliance, the love of freedom, the feeling of invincibility has never deserted the inhabitants of Arabia.

Its emigrants. The rest of the world seemed to be flowing with milk and honey to those who had been trained in such a school. Hence

Arabia's exports have included a series of conquerors, as well as a steady supply of camels and
frankincense.   If primeval history can be in-
ferred from the affinities of language, the ancestral
home of the undivided Semites—the cradle of the
Assyrians, Aramæans, Hebrews, Phœnicians,
Ethiopians—may reasonably be located on the
Arabian side of the Persian Gulf.   The camel,
the ass, the dog, wheat and barley were known
and named in the parent home ; but the horse,
the cat, grapes, olives, figs, wine were met and
named differently by the separated branches of
the Semitic stock. All the languages are as
closely related as the daughters of Latin.   They
conform so consistently to one distinct type, with
roots of triple consonants, pronouns, numerals,
and verbal categories of similar structure, that
all these separate languages must have been cast
in a common mould. Hammurabi's dynasty,
which held sway in Babylonia for a thousand
years, would thus represent the first-fruits of
desert training, though they may have reached
their throne by way of Damascus.   In much
later days another migration crossed the Red
Sea into Africa ; the Ethiopic language remains
as an indication of origin and affinity.   In the
early centuries of the Christian era, Arabs
established kingdoms at Palmyra in the Syrian

desert and around Hira on the banks of the Euphrates.

Physical condition at 600 A.D.   What was the condition of Arabia when Mohammed was born in 570 A.D. ? The nomad tribes had " no dwelling but the tent, no entrenchment but the sword, no law but the traditionary song of their bards." The most that constructive skill had attempted was found in the tanks at Aden and a great reservoir at Marib. Inscriptions celebrate the repair of the Marib reservoir ; the final collapse of the dam becomes a kind of Deluge in Arab legend, and accounts for the disappearance of Saba. Hundreds of inscriptions in the Himyarite language have been deciphered in the last fifty years, and they attest a long succession of rulers both in Yemen and in North Arabia. There were few great monuments to illustrate history for future generations.

Religion and morals.   In religion the pagan Arabs were tolerant of refugees, Zoroastrian, Jewish, Christian ; and from these they learnt a little of their several beliefs. Those who are never under a roof become familiar with the stars. Sunrise and sunset, the sequence of the seasons and the constellations, the sounds of the desert had coloured the Sabæanism which formed the common religion. Many of the stars still bear the names they got in Arabia. Mohammed's maternal grandfather is said to have urged the Koreish to give exclusive devotion to Sirius. A peculiar veneration was given to the Black Stone (an irregular oval in shape, seven inches in diameter), which was built into a small stone temple, called the Ka'aba, at Mecca. Maximus of Tyre (second century A.D.) mentions the worship of this stone among the Arabs. Native legend says the stone had been white when it fell from heaven, but contact with so many sinful sons of Adam had turned it black. Mecca became a place of pilgrimage, during which there was an annual truce of several months ; and three hundred and sixty idols received the homage of the pilgrims at the Ka'aba. Tribal kinship with clear genealogies was very strong ; without it an Arab would be as defenceless as Cain. In the sacred months there were contests of the tribes for prizes in poetry and eloquence. In the other months, all travellers in the deserts were looked upon as trespassers, and had to pay for being caught in their offence. Tribal wars were numbered by hundreds, and arose on the most trifling provocations. Where life is hard for all, mercy is not easy for any. Perhaps the darkest blemish of the Times of Ignorance, as the Arabs call the centuries before their Prophet, was the exposure of female infants. " The best son-in-law is the grave."

Jews.   Jewish immigrants were settled in some strength at Yathrib and at other stations on the trade routes. They appear to have made some converts among different tribes ; and a vague knowledge of Jewish tradition, especially about Ishmael, is found among the more curious Arabs. Yosef Dhu Nowas, the ruler of Yemen about 520 A.D., adopted Judaism so seriously that he sought to impose it by force on everybody on pain of being thrown into a fiery furnace ; he thus earned for himself the nickname, " The Lord of the Pit."

Christians.   Christianity also had only touched the surface of life in Arabia. " Arabians " are mentioned at Pentecost (Acts 2[11]) ; and St. Paul lived for some time under the Arabian King Arethas, whose dominion included Damascus. The Arab was not impressed by ornate buildings or pompous embassies. But when he found a lonely hermit, artificially cultivating more hardship than the desert itself imposed, he felt that such a spirit was in earnest. We read of a St. Saba, called the Star of Palestine, who once shared all his scanty food with starving Bedouin ; and ever afterwards the grateful tribesmen kept the hermit well supplied. The reckless generosity of the Arab invented something original when it became Christian. His Arabian birth and blood are probably responsible for the performance of Simeon Stylites, " who stood upright on a pillar 22 cubits high for five years." Simeon's preaching won him fame and followers among his kinsmen. From this source an ascetic type of Christian practice may have influenced the Hanifi or Puritans who welcomed Mohammed in Medina.

Abraha of Yemen. The titles and dioceses attributed to Frumentius and Theophilus, in the time of Athanasius and onwards, were probably more nominal than real. In the time of Justinian (527–565 A.D.) the evidence for Christianity in Arabia becomes more definite. Dhu Nowas was dethroned in Yemen ; his place was taken by a Christian ruler, Abraha, viceroy for Abyssinia. One of Abraha's inscriptions from 543 A.D. invokes " Rahman, the Merciful One, and His Messiah, and the Holy Spirit." Justinian hoped that Yemen would protect the caravans bringing silk from China against Persian attack ; and he sent an important embassy to the Negus of Abyssinia, as intermediary with Yemen. The Negus came forth in his State chariot drawn by four elephants, and gave audience to the am-bassadors in the open air. A friendly arrange-ment was made, but had little success against the Persians. It was silk rather than religion that interested these high contracting parties. Abraha of Yemen was more in earnest for his Christian faith. He had built a cathedral in Yemen, and hoped to attract the Arabs to his capital as a centre for pilgrims. Good preaching might appeal to those who listened with keen interest to recitations of original poetry ; Mohammed himself referred with respect to the preaching of Coss, bishop of Najran. But Abraha perceived that the attraction of Mecca was strong ; so he equipped a large army, accompanied by an elephant—a novelty in Arabia—and set out to destroy the Ka'aba. " If that were done," he announced to the Meccans, " he would retire without shedding the blood of any man." The Koreish resisted this demand, but could not check the invader. A plague of small-pox or some mysterious visitation saved the Ka'aba and ruined the expedition of " the Elephant," as the Arabs call it. This happened in the year 570 A.D., in which year also Mohammed was born. The spiritual heritage into which he was born thus included an immemorial star-worship and idolatry, legendary Jewish traditions, and inadequate representations of an ambiguous Christianity. So far as alien faiths are concerned, Mohammed's primary inspiration is independent and original. His faith was created within his own spirit, and depended little on human assistance or spiritual inheritance.

Biography of Mohammed. The outward events of Mohammed's career require to be shortly recalled before considering his spiritual achievement. Born three months after his father's death, he lost his mother also, at the age of six. Two years later the child had again to know the grief of bereavement when his grandfather died. His uncle, Abu Talib, adopted the orphan, and at sore cost discharged the duties of next-of-kin. His Bedouin nurse, the slave woman he inherited, and all who had to do with him, seem to have liked the little boy; and when he grieved that his uncle was going away to Syria, the uncle agreed to let the lad of twelve years come with the caravan. Though of noble blood, the family was poor; and Mohammed did his share of service as shepherd and obliging helper in the humblest work. When he reached the age of twenty-five his uncle told him of a chance of earning four camels by becoming assistant caravan conductor. Mohammed joined the company, and would have a chance of seeing all sorts and conditions of men on the way to Syria. The journey was successful; and the widow Khadijah, to whom the enterprise belonged, arranged to marry Mohammed, who was her junior by fifteen years. Their married life was happy, and several children were born to them.

Known as el-Amin. Two incidents of the next fifteen years deserve mention. The sacred Ka'aba required repair, and four families were disputing as to who should have the honour of replacing the Black Stone in the wall. To avoid a quarrel, they agreed to invite the first man who chanced to enter the courtyard to place the Stone in its position. It was Mohammed, or el-Amin—the trustworthy as he was called—who first appeared. He laid his square garment on the ground, placed the Sacred Stone upon it, and bade each family lift a corner of the robe to the proper height; then he fixed the Stone in its due place in the wall. The art of conciliation in this trifle would command veneration in Arabia equal to the respect given to courage in war. The other incident of his pre-prophetic days was the formation of a band of men to protect the victims of lawless aggressors. No chief at Mecca had power enough at the time to punish robbery or assault, if the family to which the offender belonged overlooked his offence. Right had disarmed itself; violence was safe and profitable. The league of honest men was formed to trace and punish the offenders, and to make restitution to those who were injured. In later life Mohammed used to say : " I would not exchange for the choicest camel in all Arabia the remembrance of being present at the oath which we took . . . to stand by the oppressed " (*Oath of Fudhul*).

His conversion. The call to prophecy came to Mohammed when he was about forty years of age. His own perception of truth was separated by two or three years from his feeling of the necessity laid upon him to arise and warn others. Until he was clear in his own soul he shrank from inviting others to share his experience. His wife Khadijah, his slave and friend Zaid, his adopted son Ali, his intimate friend Abu Bekr, were the first to encourage him to obey the Voice that spoke to his spirit. One of his converts, Arqam, gave his house near the Ka'aba as a place for prayer and mutual consultation. The Meccans in general despised the enthusiast, and resented his criticism of the holy things of their fathers. They spoke to Abu Talib, Mohammed's protector by blood, who had not become a Moslem, asking him to silence his nephew. " Though they gave me the Sun in my right hand," said Mohammed, " and the Moon in my left, to bring me back from my undertaking, yet will I not pause till the Lord carry my cause to victory, or till I die for it." Thereupon he burst into tears and turned to leave his kinsman.   Abu Talib called him back and said : " Go in peace, son of my brother ; and say what thou wilt ; for, by God, I will on no condition abandon thee."   At great cost in inclination and in life Abu Talib loyally fulfilled his promise to the end.

Opposition.   Humbler Moslems with less powerful patrons had to leave Mecca, and about a hundred found refuge with the Christians of Abyssiania (616 A.D.).   Two influential converts, Omar, afterwards Khalif, and Hamza, joined the Moslems, and they insisted on saying their prayers at the Ka'aba itself, despite the idols. The whole family of Hashim, though mostly non-Moslem, were excommunicated by the rest of the city because they refused to abandon their kinsman.   The result of ten years' preaching (610–620 A.D.) in Mecca had been to enlist about 200 fervent converts, and to excite indignant opposition in the other 10,000 inhabitants of the city.   Mohammed then visited Tayif (620 A.D.), but was repulsed with open hostility.   With pilgrims from Medina he was more successful. Among them certain Hanifs were disaffected to the current idolatry, and ready to welcome a more reasonable faith.   Twelve of them gave their pledge in these terms : " To have no God but Allah, to withhold their hand from what was not their own, to flee fornication, not to kill newborn infants, to shun slander, and to obey God's messenger as far as was fairly to be asked." This was called the Women's Oath, and those who took it were able to muster seventy-three men and two women from Medina by the pilgrimage in March 622.

Mecca became more hostile, Medina more friendly. The Prophet transferred one hundred and fifty of his converts to Medina from Mecca; and he was soon obliged to follow. He and Abu Bekr were pursued with deadly intent, and had to remain in hiding in the cave of Mount Thaur. We are but two, and our enemies are many, thought Abu Bekr. "Think not thus, Abu Bekr!" said the Prophet; "we are two, but God is in the midst, a Third." Some have ascribed to the Prophet a subtle design of creating an empire by any serviceable means; it would be as reasonable to ascribe to St. Andrew a secret purpose of conquering Scotland when he produced the loaves and the fishes. Mohammed was in direct obedience from day to day to the Divine Voice which was guiding him.

The Moslem era begins. The Flight from Mecca to Medina is the beginning of the new era, called the Hejira. It began on the 20th June 622 A.D., and reckons years by the Moon instead of the

Sun, so that 15th March 1923 A.D. corresponds to the 27 Ragab 1341 A.H. of the Moslem calendar. At Medina, when the Prophet arrived, two factions were contending for the vacant headship of the city ; and various disputes were referred to the Prophet, whose decisions commanded general assent. The zeal of the converts gained adherents rapidly, and the daily prayers were carried out without hindrance. The opposition of influential Jews required Mohammed to consider Biblical traditions and to define his own independent teaching. In saying their prayers the Moslems had hitherto turned their faces toward Jerusalem ; now they were required to choose the angle which directed their eyes toward Mecca. The choice of Friday for common public worship may have been intended to divide Moslems from Jews and Christians who observed Saturday and Sunday. Bells on churches had their counterpart in the Muezzin who called the hours of prayer from the minaret.

Moslem brotherhood. The Moslems of Medina were knit by a new bond, which cancelled the tribal kinship of blood. " Every Moslem was every Moslem's brother." The old loyalty, which required all members of a tribe to unite for defence against enemies, was transferred to Islam for defence against idolaters. The Meccans were still at war against Mohammed and his followers, and the new fellowship did not hesitate to defend themselves. A thousand Meccans **Battles.** came to Bedr, near Medina, and were defeated by Mohammed with 300 men (624 A.D., A.H. 2). Another battle took place at Ohod (625) in which the Prophet was wounded but not defeated. The Jews organised a coalition of some 10,000 opponents of Islam and besieged Medina ; but by skilful entrenchments the defenders won this War of the Fosse (627 A.D., A.H. 5). The Meccans became less anxious for fighting, and agreed by the convention of Hadaibiya (A.H. 6) to let Mohammed come unarmed to keep the pilgrimage at Mecca in the following year. In retaliation for the War of the Fosse, Mohammed defeated the Jews of Khaibar and treated some of them with great severity (A.H. 7). They had taken the aggressive in war and had been defeated ; but they should not be called martyrs in consequence. Dhu Nowas, the Jewish ruler of Yemen, had been much more severe ; Abraha, the Christian, had attacked Mecca for religious reasons ; the offer of mercy by Mohammed, on condition that the Jews should accept Islam, was an advance on the humanity that was current at the time. In January of 630 A.D. Mohammed marched against Mecca with 10,000 men; the city surrendered without fighting, and the inhabitants were surprised that Mohammed

Surrender of Mecca, 630 A.D
forgave his persecutors without exacting vengeance. What he insisted on was the solemn destruction of the three hundred and sixty idols of the Ka'aba. Being now master of Mecca, the Prophet received embassies and deputations from all parts; in two years the southern and eastern provinces of Arabia had accepted the teachers of the new religion, and had pledged their loyalty to the Prophet. The Farewell Pilgrimage from Medina to Mecca took place in March 630 A.D. With vast crowds of enthusiastic worshippers all the ceremonies were performed by the Prophet as he meant them to be observed in time to come. In addressing the people Mohammed said : " Truly Satan despaireth of being worshipped in your land for ever. Verily I have fulfilled my mission. I have left that amongst you—a plain command, the Book of God, and manifest ordinances—which, if ye hold fast, ye shall never go astray." " O Lord, I have delivered my message and discharged my ministry; O Lord, I beseech Thee, bear Thou witness unto it." His death took place at Medina in June 632 A.D. In less than a generation, disunited Arabia had been fused by religious fervour into new life. No minorities

were left ; idolatry never showed itself again, the whole peninsula had experienced " the expulsive power of a new affection."

Is Mohammed a prophet ? What made Mohammed a prophet and how were men moved to give obedience to his words ? What made Amos or Isaiah or St. Peter or St. Paul commanders of the souls of men ? In all these cases a human soul, living like others in its own image, becomes gradually conscious of a new Personality. They feel that a Living Being is speaking to their spirit, guiding their intelligence, stirring their emotions, generating a deep concern for the good of their kind, making them feel the difference between what ought to be and what is. The human character of these prophets is strongly marked, and each has his own. Amos is stern, Isaiah majestic, Jeremiah sensitive, Peter impetuous, Paul self-assertive ; yet all agree in the quality of the reverence they pay to the Divine Personality who speaks to and through them. They all know that there can be no divided allegiance in the service of God ; their first conviction is that God is One, that there is a clear distinction between right and wrong, and that God's purpose is to establish right among men. Personal experience and the test of time verified and vindicated the Divine authority of the message of the Prophets and Apostles.

The nature of his call. Applying similar criteria to the Prophet of Arabia, it is evident that he had no human tutors more than his neighbours had had for a century. It was no scholar's research on ancient books that lit the fire in his soul. The tenor of his life for forty years shows a modest conformity to the good side of current custom with a silent process of deep reflection. He welcomes solitude ; and, latterly, seeks for it habitually amid the desolate and inhuman rocks of Mount Hira. What he thought and felt may have been put into words, as Amos, watching his sheep near the Dead Sea, made fragments of poetry to express what he felt. Gradually Mohammed became conscious that the solitude could speak, and soliloquy became dialogue. What words were used, when human language was facing the ineffable, could not convey to others all that inspiration meant to the Prophet. His resolute rationalism asserted itself even when spiritual constraint seemed irresistible. His neighbours believed in a hierarchy of spirits, jinns, demons, angels who strove to dominate our souls for good or evil. Rather than say one word falsely in the name of Allah, he was more than once ready to cast himself headlong from

the rocks and thus to end his spiritual struggle.
How could the solitary mystic in the cave of Hira
be sure that the Voice which bade him speak
in the name of Allah was not a jinn or a demon ?
" Nay," said his wife, Khadijah, " it cannot be
so. For you are kind to your relatives ; you speak
the truth ; you are faithful in trust ; you bear
the afflictions of the people ; you spend in good
works what you gain in trade ; you are hospitable ; and you assist your fellow-men." Mohammed felt the burden of what was irrational and
absurd around him ; he was driven to the conviction that the three hundred idol-deities of
the Arabians were fictions of the imagination,
" nought but names," false because non-existent.
The certainty that God is One, that the souls of
men must stand before the Judgment-seat of God, is
the result of his inspiration and becomes his message
to his contemporaries. By his intense sincerity, by
his carefulness to recall concessions which he had
seemed to make of his own impulse without Divine
authority, by his life and teaching in Mecca, by the
substance of his message, this great Arabian has
similar claims with Amos to be called a Prophet.
The philosophical theist may accept, as Gibbon
declares, the simple and rational piety he inculcates:

      " La ilaha illa 'llahi,
       Wa Muhammadu Rasuluhu."

The Koran. Jews and Christians were honoured above others by Mohammed, because God had sent them true prophets and a sacred Book. But Moslems never gave the deep deference to the Bible which Christians had shown towards the Old Testament. Like St. Paul, the Koran finds the faith of Abraham a truer foundation for the religious temperament than the later Mosaic code. Tradition described Abraham's rejection of polytheism in terms which corresponded to the mental process of Mohammed. The story of Hagar in the wilderness, going aside that she might not see her little boy, Ishmael, dying of thirst, threw light upon the distant past; and suggested an origin for the sacred well, Zemzem, at Mecca. The Prophet sometimes referred to Islam as a republication of the faith of Abraham; and the Moslems gladly acknowledged Abraham as the fountain of their blood and the model of magnanimity. The Koran consists entirely of the words of Mohammed; Ayesha was quite right when she said: " The Prophet's disposition is no other than the Koran itself." The collection was made, not by Mohammed himself, but by his secretary, Zaid, within a year after the Prophet's death. To prevent various readings in different copies, the Khalif Othman prepared a standard copy (A.H. 30,

651 A.D.), which remains authoritative till to-day. "There is probably in the world no other work which has remained twelve centuries with so pure a text." Any alteration of a word became an offence against the State.

How com-piled. Poetry in Arabia had been recited and remembered, rarely written and read. The Suras, as the chapters of the Koran are called, were revealed at different times during twenty-two years, and were known to many by heart. Zaid collected them from palm-leaves and tablets; and also from the breasts of men. The parts used in prayer were familiar to all; promotion in the army was sometimes settled by advancing the man who knew most of the Koran by heart. Zaid did not arrange the chapters according to the dates of their origin; and the modern reader, ignorant of the contemporary history, encounters prayer, argument from legend, poetry, admonition, soliloquy, and legal regulations, with no pervasive scheme of time or logic. When read in the order of delivery the first group is seen to consist of short pieces, describing self-communings, invocations of the Power of God as seen in nature, aspiration, awe of Divine Judgment. The next group becomes more didactic, appeals to men to forsake their errors and to obey the call of God. More notice is now taken of Jewish and Christian traditions. The last group of twenty-nine chapters announced at Medina, are longer and less poetical in substance. Mohammed had become a Judge, an Army Commander, a Legislator; his announcements are more in the form of Army Orders, though they use similar forms with the earliest Suras. The student of religion finds it less easy to give the same degree of inspiration to the Medina chapters as to the earlier. Many decisions were made for local and temporary conditions, and therefore lose universal validity. In particular, the legislation and practice of the Prophet in regard to marriage laws — although these, too, were an improvement on preceding usage — might be adjusted in theory to the practice which prevails among the vast majority of Moslems to-day. Read in English, the Koran has been pronounced uninteresting; read in Arabic, the diligent foreigner begins to understand why the native Arabian finds in it a superhuman excellence and beauty. To please the indolent imagination was never the purpose of this Book. The *Manual of Infantry Training* is also uninteresting to read. But the *Manual* makes blind multitudes into orderly armies, obedient to the clear purpose of a single spirit. Such, too, is the merit of the Koran.

Creed and practice. The Creed of Islam has two articles : " There is no god but Allah," and " Mohammed is a prophet of God." There are four standard duties : 1. Prayer ; 2. Almsgiving ; 3. Fasting ; 4. Pilgrimage to Mecca (if possible, once in a lifetime at least). The Prophet's own experience as an orphan taught him the worth of human compassion ; his own spiritual struggles had discovered the necessity of Divine communion, therefore he prescribed Prayer ; his observation of human nature in himself and his neighbours had taught him the difficulty of self-governance. It is interesting to find the same three prescriptions for the health of human nature in the Sermon on the Mount, and something similar in a saying of Shim'eon ha-Saddiq (200 B.C.). Man cannot ignore God without loss ; he dare not disregard the need of his neighbour ; and each man has a task within, which he must fulfil for himself as no outside power can ever do it for him.

Total abstainers. The success of Islam in persuading its adherents to abstain from the use of wine is a notable achievement. The vine grows well in many parts of Arabia, and grapes, both fresh and dried, are a valuable element of food. The pre-Islamic poets sing the praise of wine ; as allegorical heretics like Omar Khayyam did in later centuries. Persia had no aversion to stimulants; and universal custom made Arabia, like other places, liable to excess in the use of intoxicants. The climate in itself engenders a thirst which is fierce, blistering, irresistible. How did the Prophet succeed in such conditions in founding a society of total abstainers, numbered by scores of millions and lasting over a thousand years? The Koran has no emphatic imperative on the subject. " They will ask thee concerning wine and games of chance. Say: In both is great sin and advantage also to men; but their sin is greater than their advantage " (*Sura* ii. 219). " Will ye not therefore abstain from them? " (*Sura* v. 92). The blind appetites which arise from the senses, the instinctive desires which are congenital, have all to be directed by the reason and will of the individual himself. A famine may impose starvation; but that is not fasting, because it does not proceed from the volition of the individual. A majority in any community may impose certain kinds of abstinence; but that is not temperance, because it is not governance by self of what is peculiar to the self. Reason by itself is often insufficient to restrain the appetites from satisfying themselves, although reason clearly foresees the disastrous effects of indulgence. By appealing in the name of Allah to the voluntary choice of his adherents,

Mohammed succeeded where many zealous agencies have failed. The secret of success appears to lie in the discipline of fasting. Any stranger who has tried to observe the hunger-stricken Ramazan, will never accuse Islam of pandering to the appetites of sense. In a land where starvation is always imminent, the people were called to strenuous exercises for the mastery of hunger. "Fasting is for God alone, and He will give its rewards." "Utter no bad words, nor argue, nor retort to abuse" during this exercise. The will power of the Moslem was so developed in his contest with the pangs of hunger that his wholesome triumph over wine became an assured success.

Islam in action. Books tell us much about the great religions, and the test of a thousand years reveals their several qualities. But a distant foreigner, presented with our English Bible and Hymnaries, would be dismayed on discovering our Criminal Statistics. There is generally a great difference between man as he is and man as his religion says he ought to be. It is, therefore, an advantage in judging a religion to see it in action, and to compare its ideal with its actual achievement. Five years' residence in Constantinople in daily contact with its diverse races and creeds, and four years with an Army fighting against the Turks and their allies, supplied the writer with the means of judging the Moslem religion by its fruits ; and his experience during these years is the chief determinant of his conclusions.

In Constantinople. The heavy manual labour of the Turkish capital is done by Moslems, and the stranger is surprised to find the burden-bearer strictly sober and ready to say his prayers. The hard-working man, when the hour comes, will quietly enter a mosque with scores of others, high and low ; or all by himself he may pause for three minutes to pray, as he is digging a drain on a hillside. The Moslem craftsman is patient and diligent with a skill of his own, and is content with a price which the non-Moslem middleman doubles whenever he can. Kindness to animals, horses, donkeys, dogs, pigeons, is required by religion, and has become innate among Moslems. Killing of birds for amusement seemed incredible to some who read about the fate of the grouse in Scotland. The ablutions prescribed before prayer have inspired cleanliness in the humblest houses and care in preparation of food. The theory of polygamy, which diverges so strongly from Christian feeling, provides all women with family protection ; and the moral degradation of great European cities has no equivalent among Moslem women. The Moslem resents irreverence in tourists who insist on visiting mosques; but he scrupulously respects the sanctity of church and synagogue. What he demands for his own religion, he is ready to give to others. Feeling is too intense to contemplate attempts at proselytising; but mutual respect led to interchange of esteem and friendship. Genuine good character in Jew, Christian, or Moslem commanded respect from them all. There is a true democratic element in Islam; the negro and the Pasha are equal, and feel themselves equal, in the mosque. The fine deference of officials to their superiors, of a son to his father or elder brother, rests on the common assurance that the superior is only a servant of Allah, who is Master of them all. At a country village like Bunarbashi, the fifty men were full of eager curiosity to see the strangers who had come to examine Trojan ruins; but dignity and courtesy forbade any intrusion, or any charge for undeserved hospitality.

Ramazan. No description of Ramazan can do justice to its effect on half a million souls who have completed that month of bodily discipline. From sunrise to sunset every Moslem has forbidden himself the use of food, water, tobacco. On the Night of Power, towards the end of Ramazan, the men gather in the mosques for common worship. The mosque of the Agia Sophia—formerly the Church of the Holy Wisdom—had about three thousand men devoutly worshipping at that service in 1900. The fasting by day had provided a spiritual exaltation in every individual; the prayers expressed adoration, penitence, consecration to God. The collective suggestion becomes all-powerful, and the spiritual result incalculable. Every gesture, every utterance of these worshippers confessed that " God is a Spirit, and they that worship him must worship him in Spirit and in truth." Judged by its fruits, Islam can claim a power over its adherents and a pervasive influence on their lives which contemporary systems attain only among their most zealous groups.

Does War produce results like Islam ? The expansion of Islam requires notice in order to test the hypothesis that this religion owes its propagation to the sword. In thirty years Arabia had been made one in spirit by religion ; and though for a moment, when the Prophet died, the old discords threatened to revive, the new faith made unity permanent. Within a century Moslem arms had conquered half the known world and ruled from Samarkand to Gibraltar. Alexander the Great had conquered his world, but his empire fell into fragments when he died. When Moslem

military power became weaker, their religion
went on making fresh converts. Seldom do
Moslems change their faith for another, never
on a national scale. Islam displaced the religion
of the Magi in Persia and extended its influence
in Central Asia. The ten million converts in
China have been made without support from
military power. It would have been easy to
exert political pressure in India; yet the seventy
million Indian Moslems were won by the appeal
to heart and mind. In Java, in Africa, Islam has
spread with no assistance from military power.
Careful computation places the number of
Moslems at 201 millions in all; and no one
can believe that war can make or retain a
fellowship such as this. The real inference
from the rapid conquests of the first century is,
that, if an army has a religion which it seriously
believes, its power is marvellously multiplied.
The Moslem victors were deeply religious men;
they were missionaries unconsciously by the
intensity of their belief. The Moslem trader
speaks of his religion as occasion offers; and
without systematic organisation he succeeds in
diffusing his religion. A Moslem, who was
condemned to death in the Belgian Congo, is
reported to have spent his last hours in trying
to convert the Christian missionary who was

sent to minister to his spirit. Each man has an individual obligation to invite strangers to share his faith ; and many put it in practice.

Intellectual stimulus. Religious revival is often followed by fresh intellectual energy, and this was the case with Islam. For four centuries secular knowledge at its best found more hospitality among Moslems than among contemporary Christians. Philosophy, which had been dumb since Greek was forgotten, now found her voice again in the Arabic language. Ibn Khaldun lays down the rules for writing history as clearly as Thucydides or Tacitus ; and his criticism of the Pentateuch anticipates the discoveries of Robertson Smith and Wellhausen. Such effects are not secured by the use of the sword. Under Christian influences the West in more recent times resorts to war with the deepest regret in the last extremity only. Islam, from its birth, had to fight for self-preservation ; it accepts war as it accepts pestilence or famine, as something which cannot be avoided. Even a Pagan Arab—Murra of Shaiban (*c.* 500 A.D.)—maintained that forbearance to those who have committed crimes is merely inviting further crimes. " Through war thou mayest win to peace, when good is tried in vain." The same principle pervades the Koran ; militant action is permitted only as the one means to attain the end of peace—submission to God, as the very name " Islam " signifies. Nations called Christian are driven to a similar justification for war; agnosticism has made them less confident in asserting the will of God; and in case they may be wrong, our British battle-cry has become, " Let God defend the right."

Bolshevism. The call to hatred and destruction which has lately emanated from Russia invites the workers of all lands to share its authors' hatred and follow their example. " We must educate the labouring masses of the East to hatred, to the will to fight the whole of the rich classes indifferently, whoever they may be." Thus spoke Zinoviev to a congress of 1900 delegates at Baku, September 1920. Capitalism does not alarm the Moslem, because the love of inordinate wealth has never been his failing. On his death-bed Mohammed inquired whether the half-dozen dinars in the house had been given away, and ordered their instant distribution. " Could he enter the presence of the Divine Judge having left so much power for relieving need unused ? " That was the meaning of Death Duties for the Prophet of Arabia. Wealth for his followers meant power for beneficence; relief of distress was a standard imperative duty.

Usury was abhorrent; and Moslem millionaires are almost unknown to history. The call to hate from Russia will have little success among Moslems; and God-fearing men everywhere may rejoice that Islam offers so strong a bulwark against general anarchy.

Islam deserves to be studied. British Christians owe to themselves and to Islam the duty of understanding the rise and progress of this religion. Our circle of knowledge welcomes information about ancient Crete and Egypt, about primitive customs from New Guinea or Thibet. There is a richer intellectual stimulus in appreciating the spiritual forces that emerged from Arabia, captured and held the devotion of so many diverse races, and are still throbbing with vitality. As British citizens, we are linked with seventy million Moslems in the fellowship of our commonwealth of nations; and their spiritual ideals would act as a wholesome tonic to our own. Any reader of Sir William Muir's *Life of Mahomet* and *Annals of the Caliphate*, where good and bad are frankly recorded, will be convinced that they were great spirits who called Islam into being; it will become clear why Carlyle found " The Hero as Prophet " in Arabia.

> " Now were not hate man's natural element,
> Churches and Mosques had risen side by side."

Who best can show nobility ? So said Mutanabbi of Aleppo (965 A.D.). The apostles of hate can only make disciples who will hate and destroy their teachers. Reverence for noble natures doing noble deeds is the right basis for friendship. From the dawn of history there comes to us a picture of Abraham at Salem offering homage to Melchizedek, the priest of the Most High God. When Jerusalem peacefully capitulated to the Moslems (636 A.D.), the Khalif Omar rode from Medina to make terms with Sophronius, the Christian Patriarch. The Patriarch and the Khalif happened to be in the Church of the Holy Sepulchre when the Moslem hour of prayer arrived. Omar went outside and performed his devotions in the open air, explaining to the Patriarch that he had done so, lest his followers in time to come might claim to pray within the church. Omar pledged the Moslems to respect the sanctity of the church, a pledge which has been loyally kept for 1200 years. Omar's magnanimity has recently been repeated. When a British General was called upon to enter the Holy City, he did so, constrained by the grace of our own religion, modestly and reverently. His first care was that the Dome of the Rock—the Mosque of Omar as it is often called—should be scrupulously respected ; and he appointed Moslem soldiers from his Indian Army to this congenial duty. Thus nobility evokes nobility across the millenniums ; and all good souls are united by respect for wisdom and magnanimity.

LECTURE VI.

THE HERITAGE AND OBLIGATIONS OF SEMITIC RELIGION.

Semitic interest in history. UNIVERSAL history shrinks into small dimensions when we deduct that sphere which is involved in the survey of the Semitic religions. The rest of the ancient world had little to say for themselves ; their testimony, so far as it escaped oblivion, survived in its own region, but failed to captivate the attention of strangers yet to be. Half the human race to-day is touched by some form of the faith of Abraham ; and though the other half have many virtues of their own, they had and have a smaller share in directing the creative energies of the human race. One result peculiar to Semitic inspiration, was an activity of intellect which strove to understand as well as to remember. Intellectual curiosity in the nineteenth century of the Christian era was the same in kind as the spirit that wrote the preamble to the Bible. The modern student has been brought face to face with a magnified

12

universe, and has to make a new " Genesis " for
himself. Man has been somewhat annoyed to
discover that the cosmos went on so long without
his presence. The ancient picture of the process
of Creation had hinted that the week was nearly
finished when man was introduced on Friday
evening. There was a time when the Earth
was uninhabitable : " no plant of the field was
yet in the earth, and no herb of the field had yet
sprung up ; there was not a man to till the
ground." There was also a time, immeasurably
more remote, when the Earth itself was " without
form and void." Modern science has discovered
credible measurements and agents of change.
We can now contemplate the birth of the solar
system, the separation of the planets with their
moons or rings, the independence of our little
home the Earth. The vague intervals in the
old birth-stories of heaven and earth have become
limitless æons to modern astronomy ; and man's
insignificance in time has chilled his youthful
complacency. But the stars themselves are
always there, though fancies about them have
changed ; the old fear and worship have been
replaced by understanding and admiration. The
discovery of Neptune by the calculations of man's
mind was splendidly verified by the vision of the
eye, when the telescope was turned to a little

circle, 3000 million miles away, to await the
arrival of the invisible planet. Such a result
confirms our faith in the veracity of intelligence,
and is sufficient substitute for naive arrogance.
The extra-Semitic half of the world has often
enjoyed a serene and tranquil equilibrium ; but
the restless energy of the prophetic spirit has been
responsible for the advancement of knowledge.

Prophetic inspiration is also responsible for
an intelligent interest in the past. In considering
the modern framework for a picture of human
religion, it appeared that the testimony of the
rocks had something humbling to reveal. The
story of Eden said man looked about him and
felt lonely till other living creatures were made.
They were there for his amusement, to attract
his observation, to impel him to devise names
for them ; but he felt himself their superior,
with right of dominion over the creatures, except
his equal Eve. But man's kinship with the
animals is closer than he then suspected. In
the elements that make up his body, in the
successive phases of his bodily growth, man
follows the common path of terrestrial life. His
dust and ashes are identical with the ground ;
the handful of clay borrowed by his spirit returns
just like that of the animals to inorganic elements.
The procession of life on earth has been long and

slow.   Half the primitive races ascribe the movement to an evolution of natural potencies ;   the
rest incline to postulate a creative agency.   Man's
lease of life on earth may have extended to three
or four hundred thousand years ; but man's
memory is dead to all that happened before the
last sixty centuries.

Non-Semitic   No race has a monopoly in religion
systems.   or in language, though each may have
their own.   The capacity for religion is as widely
diffused as feeling and thought.   The belief in
spirits, the personification of natural forces, the
worship of ancestors, were earlier expressions of
the religious faculty than the devotion to national
gods, who were jealous of foreign deities.   But
very soon in history the mystic knows that religion is a matter between what is human and
what is Divine—*solus cum solo* ; tribal divisions
are irrelevant to such an experience.   The most
important non-Semitic religions include Hinduism
with some 250 million adherents.   For the Hindu,
in the abstract, the deity is impersonal.   " There
is but one Being, no second."   To the Universe
he says : " Cradle and grave art thou of all
that is."   Right and wrong are matter of con-
venience ; man's chief end is reabsorption in
this pantheistic total.   Another great religion
owes its origin to a personal founder, and numbers

500 million adherents. Buddhism is an explicit denial of theism, or perhaps a form of subconscious theism. The Buddhist Catechism declares that " a personal God is regarded by Buddhists as only a gigantic shadow, thrown upon the void of space by the imagination of ignorant men." Unsatisfied desires are the torment of humanity, and man's chief end is to extinguish desire. The death of individual aspiration reproduces a trait of placid nature, and is the highest good for man. China's many millions seem to have required fewer wars than their contemporaries for many centuries; they have made their land yield food for more men than any equal area has done. They have honoured their ancestors; and they have been efficient in providing for the needs of the body. Their practical capacity, their resolute stoicism demands respect; but their contributions to metaphysics are none. Theoretical speculation, inspiration in a religious sense, has been sedulously avoided. " The study of the supernatural is injurious indeed," said Confucius.

Hope and purpose mark the Semite. In contrast with these other great systems, the Semitic character has drawn its strength from the obedience to spiritual influences. The same heaven and earth has been shared by all men; their common experience has generated a certain agreement in moral regulations. Prohibitions of murder, assault, theft are decreed by all communities. But the Semite differs in his intense conviction of monotheism, his intolerance of absurdity, his clear definition of primal human duties, his sense of moral responsibility to the Just Judge of all the earth. Further, the Semite is so impressed with the urgency of Divine right, that he accepts the duty of warning the whole world to prepare to meet their God. Most men have been content with directing their own personal life wisely. To the inspired Semite, his own welfare is only a means to an end ; till the whole human family is delivered from sin and misery, his own welfare is incomplete. Missionary enthusiasm is a distinctive mark of the Semitic religions. Non-Semitic systems have conceived the Deity as impersonal, or morally indifferent, or non-existent ; they have secured millions of adherents, mostly in tropical regions. The inspiration of the Semite has made him active in spite of climatic conditions ; and his ideals have secured allegiance in the temperate zones of the earth. A monotheism which demands strict morals, which cares for all men, which makes active efforts for universal welfare, is the peculiar possession of Semitic religion.

Nature of prophetic inspiration. In reviewing the early religion of the Hebrews, its transformation into Judaism, its development in Christianity, the republication of the faith of Abraham in Arabia, it was maintained that the progress of religion is due to the inspiration of individual prophets. It is not from clever calculation nor from great learning that the prophets receive their illumination. Advances in knowledge can be traced from one stage to another, and the ingenuity of the discoverer can be measured and appreciated. The part of the mosquito in producing malarial fever, the method of disarming small-pox, the invention of the steam-engine are examples of intelligence mastering obscurity. But the emergence of a poet or prophet—the quality of inspiration which makes a psalm more powerful than a pyramid—cannot be explained by observing causes and effects. The cause in the one case is finite ; its action can be allowed or hindered, and the difference in effect can be observed and identified. In religion there is interaction of human and divine personality. Though it is possible to conjecture the effect of any cause on a given human agent, the non-human factor remains beyond human comprehension. The influence of the Divine Personality is real and active, and transforms human personality ; but its nature remains inscrutable even to the prophet himself.

Credo ut intelligam. The inspiration and influence of the prophets cannot be ascribed to their own powers of reasoning. Reason is the critic rather than the creator of religious enthusiasm. " The stork knoweth her times " ; she finds the way from Saxony to Rhodesia. When the right moment arrives, she returns to the old nest and begins another generation. This unerring wisdom is not the gift of reason, nor can it be improved by philosophy. Animal behaviour is the response of inward organism to outward stimulus ; and though a playful dog has obviously emotions, his reason is uncritical.

> "What dog resents,
>   That he is sent,
> To follow his own nose ? "

In man, too, there is a heritage of extra-rational life with an inertia of its own. Man's intelligence cannot control his respiration, digestion, the beating of his heart. The child lives for years by its congenital aptitudes before intelligence begins to be active. Deep thinkers are a small minority in all generations ; man is more anxious to live than to know. The emotions, the higher instincts, the imagination have more power than thought in determining the health of the soul.

It is this element in human nature that responds to the preaching of the prophet. In the prophets themselves it is intense emotion — awe, hope, reverence, love—that takes command of the will and makes the personality inflexible. Spurious enthusiasm often creates hallucination, fanaticism, grotesque absurdities. The message of the true prophet is altogether exceptional, because it is found to transcend reason and to satisfy rational criticism.

Result of inspiration. The effect of inspiration is a nobler theism and a higher conception of the duty of man. The hinterland of history presents us with mental confusion, the morality of instinct —sometimes sound and stable like that of the stork—oftener, intermingled with deadly illusions. Primitive man is frightened by the discovery of his own spirit, by perceiving that in dreams his spirit has adventures while his body lies asleep, that the spirit appears when the body it used to inhabit is dead. A spiritism arises which imputes life and sex to inanimate objects — the French and Hebrew languages have no neuter gender for their nouns—which personifies the forces of nature, resorts to human sacrifice, sorcery, necromancy, magic, and fills life with fear and folly. A modern man can hardly realise the harm of magic, polytheism, and idolatry. An English eye-witness reports that an Australian magician " pointed " his stick at the strongest man in the tribe ; and within a day the man died and fulfilled the sure expectation of the magician, the tribe, and the victim himself. Newton's *Laws of Motion* had less potency for human happiness than the Prophet Micah's gospel : " What doth the Lord require of thee, but to do justly, to love mercy, and to walk humbly with thy God." The maxims, which have become familiar and transparent truth for us, were once startling innovations ; they had to encounter violent opposition, and often secured martyrdom for their authors.

Theocratic Law.   The method by which prophetic inspiration acquires its influence in history is worthy of attention.   The spirit awakened by the Prophet in his disciples expresses itself in outward acts, in stricter conduct ; and the higher morality involves a change of custom. The distinctive acts of the new fellowship become habitual, are classified and collected into a code of obligatory law.   Reverence is transferred from the prophet to the law ; conscience and private judgment are distrusted, fresh inspiration is neither expected nor desired.   Rigid observance of law confers on a community the benefits of order, as seen in the beehive or the ant-heap.   Non-conformists must not expect toleration ; any reformer will encounter violent opposition. The Law or Book becomes a canonical imperative ; the power to modify the statutory religion is denied to its Divine Author and any future messengers from heaven.

The Spirit and the Law in Judaism, This sequence of prophecy, law, revival, and reaction has been evident in each and in all the Semitic religions. The four great Hebrew prophets of the eighth century before Christ provoked a powerful reaction under King Manasseh ; but their teaching inspired the Reformation under King Josiah (622 B.C.), and established a new version of the Mosaic Law—Deuteronomy—as the constitution of the State. The disciples of Ezekiel, who was priest as well as prophet, remembering in exile the ruins of Jerusalem, made a law of holiness for an ideal theocratic community, protected against unclean intruders, cultivating its own devotion by elaborate ceremonials. Their inspiration grew into another " Law of Holiness " ; and the earliest and latest forms of Mosaic Law were combined into the Pentateuch. Ezra and Nehemiah succeeded in investing the Five Mosaic Books with such authority that they regulated the life of the restored community in Jerusalem for five centuries, and provided Judaism with its principles till the present time.

in Chris-　　Christianity owes its existence to a
tianity,　revival of prophetic inspiration.　Within
a few centuries the Church had fixed the evangelic
temperament in a New Testament, in Creeds,
in an Imperial State religion.　After the time of
Origen it became nearly as dangerous to publish
heretical opinions as it had been in Jerusalem
under the Pharisees.　By the time of the Inquisition in Spain we see Authority in the name of
religion applying the stern principles of the Pharisees against their own lineal descendants, who
are now nonconformists, outside the sacred system
in power.

in Islam.　　In Arabia the primary reaction
against the teaching of the Prophet
was insignificant.　The Paganism that disappeared
was too irrational to attract a deeper attachment.
The new religion, born of the Spirit, at once
created a definite system of belief and practice ;
but it remained for many centuries favourable
to the exericse of thought.　Aristotle was better
known in Islam than in Christendom.　The
Khalif Ma'mun—the contemporary of Charlemagne—used to invite all the sects to friendly
banquets ;　and they found serious entertainment
in discussing the relation of man to God, the
problem of freewill, the reconciliation of faith
and reason.　Al Ma'arri, " the Dante of Persia,"

born at Aleppo (973 A.D.), resenting the theory that a sacred Book could be uncreated and eternal, maintained that reason and conscience must be satisfied in applying the Book to life.

> " And the Maker infinite,
>   Whose poem is Time,
> He need not weave in it
> A forced stale rhyme."
>   (*Translation of* R. A. NICHOLSON.)

Ibn Sina or Avicenna (980–1037 A.D.), born near Bokhara, was probably the most learned man of his time.   His deference to the Koran did not seriously restrict either his thought or his morals. His Quatrain, ascribed popularly to another source, is a fair account of his life.

> " Up from Earth's Centre through the Seventh Gate
>   I rose, and on the throne of Saturn sate ;
> And many a knot unravelled by the Road,
>   But not the Master-knot of human fate."

Of course such mobility of intelligence is exceptional ; and the orthodox elements of Islam looked on such speculations with strong disfavour. The philosopher was required to keep his fasts like other men, else his theory became suspect. So long as men said their prayers and gave alms and abstained from wine, they were free to do what they liked with hands and head.   They had the same freedom which Mohammed conceded to the gardeners who were busy artificially fertilising the palm trees to secure a crop of dates. " You know better than I do what concerns your worldly interests." In recent times there are indications of a revival of Moslem intellect. Kheir-ed-Din in his book, *The Surest Means of Knowing the State of Nations* (1860), pleads for fresh study of nature and science. He calls upon his co-religionists to renew their devotion to " justice and liberty—two things which, for Europeans, have become second nature." Islam used to be open-eyed and progressive, but it became content with passive obedience to its tradition ; Kheir-ed-Din and many others (*e.g. Notes on Islam*, by Sir Ahmed Hussain, 1922) are now intent on following the active spirit of the early centuries. The impetus of Western thought on Japanese tradition resulted in a remarkable renaissance ; in Islam there is a past achievement and example, which did not exist in the case of Japan, which justify high hopes of good from fresh activity of the Moslem intellect.

The Scrip-   The Sacred Books of the Semites—
  tures.   the Bible and the Koran—are an important contribution to civilisation. They have already exerted a powerful influence on history ; they cannot cease to remain a treasure in the future. As books, they differ in origin from

general literature. The greatest Prophets spoke to hearers ; they themselves did not write books for readers. The hearers of the Divine Word recognised its power ; but the Prophet had passed away before his words were gathered into a sacred book. The literature is only a dim reflection of the inspired life. The collectors of prophetic utterances felt too deep reverence to allow them to be critical editors. Pentateuch, Gospels, Koran suffer, as books, from the casual arrangement of their materials. In spite of this the reader who sincerely seeks Divine guidance has seldom failed to find it. It has frequently happened that the adoration due to God alone has been transferred to the book which intimates His will to men. Excessive reverence has sometimes produced Bibliolatry. The revelation of God in nature is long prior in time to the making of books ; this revelation is universal in its appeal, and never ceases to affect every human soul. The human spirit in itself is a reflection of the Divine image, and there is a revelation of God through the conscience. The course of history is another revelation of the methods of Divine Providence. When the Sacred Scripture is arbitrarily exalted above these other channels of Divine Revelation, theories of verbal inspiration do violence to the tenor of the Scriptures themselves. The letter is caused to kill, and takes the place of the Spirit which maketh alive. But the testimony of God in nature, conscience, and history can be corrected and verified by the written Scriptures ; and the devout reader is conscious that he can attain to governance both by the written Word and by the Living Spirit of God.

Value. The fruitful use of the Sacred Scripture arises by obedience in the first place, and also through a genuine effort to understand them in all sincerity and honesty. The teacher of religion cannot be content with the idle repetition of familiar texts ; he must feel afresh the reasons which vindicate the truth of the text. The mental and moral process, which made the hearers of the Prophets into disciples, the motives which influenced the narrators of prophetic utterances must be fully appreciated by the interpreter of Scripture. The Bible must be allowed to tell its own story in its own way ; its quality of inspiration reveals itself to the simple hearer and also to the critical student. " He who has lost his God may find Him again in these ancient Scriptures."

General interest. As manuals for information about antiquity the Semitic Scriptures are and must remain pre-eminent authorities. Till recently they were the only audible voice from primeval times. First among men the Semite refused to forget his fathers ; filial affection taught him to appreciate and to remember the virtues of his ancestors. He told his story in such a way that strangers in all generations heard it gladly ; the majestic hieroglyphics of the Pharaohs were forgotten even by their own descendants. A modern excavation is assured of success, if it produce some reference to any one mentioned in the Bible. When George Smith in 1872 detected among the material sent from Nineveh a fragment of a tablet which referred to birds being sent forth from an ark upon the waters, London straightway sent an expedition to look for the missing pieces among the ruins of Assur-banipal's Library. Hammurabi of Babylon was indentified with the Amraphel of Genesis ; and the genial features of that ancient monarch became familiar in the illustrated newspapers. The world rejoices to hear something new about an old familiar friend. Mycenæ and Crete attract a select and learned curiosity ; but Greek wisdom appeals to a narrower circle.

Diffusion. The extensive distribution of the Bible and the Koran at the present time is creating a temperament favourable to general conciliation. No other books have been so care-

fully preserved, so often reproduced, so con-
scientiously used, so resolutely studied. Their
influence has permeated the Laws of Nations,
and has created a moral consensus of a cosmo-
politan character. Versions of the Bible have
established a classical model for many of the
languages into which they have been adequately
translated. About five hundred languages have
this one Book in common ; and scores of millions
of copies every year are attracting new readers.
Men may read to doubt or read to scorn ; but
they are using a common textbook of history and
tradition. By its sacred Books, Semitic religion
thus affords an instrument which may be used
for friendly study, for mutual understanding and
respect.

Fresh inter-   The Bible and the Koran are in
pretation. themselves a great inheritance, but
they impose great obligations on their interpreters. The latest expositor of the Koran says :
" The present tendency of the Muslim theologians
to regard the commentaries of the Middle Ages
as the final word on the interpretation of the
Holy Qur-án is very injurious, and practically
shuts out the great treasures of knowledge which
an exposition of the Holy Book in the new light
reveals " (Maulvi Muhammad Ali, *The Holy
Qur-án*, p. xcv ; 1917). Men knew less geography

and history when the Bible was written than schools are teaching to-day. The child opens its eyes upon this wonderful world, and calls for a hundred explanations. He gives those who have been here before him no rest till they have told him all they can. A century ago the Mother's Catechism made everything easy from the Bible; but the modern parent makes evasions and the child becomes a higher critic.

The Flood. Take, for example, the story of Noah's ark and the Deluge. Two inconsistent traditions have been dovetailed into one another by an editor. Each of the independent traditions accepts the common belief that there really had been a great Flood long ago, and they suppose that the whole area known to them was covered by it. The narrators of the two traditions both believe in monotheism. Therefore the Deity must have caused, or at least permitted, the Deluge. Such a decision in God or in man demands explanation. A reason is found in the cruelty of the antediluvians; the one family was spared because Noah was a righteous man, attaining the highest moral standard of his age. Both contributors to the Flood-Story are dubious whether they have succeeded in vindicating the ways of God to man. Both dismiss the troublesome tradition with a firm promise, that in the

education of the human race the method of extermination will never be tried again. By every
seedtime and harvest, by the rainbow in the sky,
men may be assured that God's mercy endureth
for ever. The Chaldæan parallel story had
misgivings about the theism of the story. Ishtar
the goddess, whose necklace was the rainbow,
and Ea remonstrate with Bel on the clumsiness
of his method, which destroyed the innocent and
guilty all together. It would have been better
to send wild beasts, or famine or pestilence.
This section of Genesis is entirely discordant
with evangelic theism. Those upon whom the
tower of Siloam fell were not sinners more than
others. Does not the rain, like the mercy of
Heaven, fall upon the unjust as well as the just ?
Floods happen still, and, like the thunderbolt,
may cause death ; but the death is not caused
by the direct volition of an angry deity. History
misconceived, involves a misrepresentation of the
Divine attributes. The interpreters of our Sacred
Books require to deliver the ingenuous youth of
to-day from the chaos which arises from teaching
him the verified secular knowledge of our own
time, and asking him to find supreme truth
commingled with the imperfect information of
antiquity. The questions of the Zulu impelled
the honest candour of Bishop Colenso to under-

take a splendid service for Christendom. The youth can easily be made susceptible to the influence of the Holy Spirit ; and, like the prophets, he will find, according to his own capacity, that Divine Communion in the present renders the past and future of the material universe a matter of secondary concern. He will also learn to appreciate the solicitude of the ancient narrators who were quite right in warning us to avoid cruelty, because cosmic changes might end our opportunities for kindliness. The advent of another glacial epoch, which is foreshadowed for the Northern Hemisphere, would confirm the moral inference from the Deluge, although it would not require from the Prophets the same theistic explanation.

Science and religion. The value of modern Science for the health of the soul may easily be overrated. Many noble characters have lived and died in healthy ignorance of recent discoveries. It was commonly believed that water and air were primal elements, the source of life and breath, incapable of dissolution or re-creation. It was then made clear that the minutest specimen of water is not a unit, but a trinity of mysterious atoms, two being of one kind requiring a new name " hydrogen," the other of a diverse kind called " oxygen." It was found that air, too, was compounded of mixed materials, one of them being the same oxgyen that helps to make up water. The indivisible atom then reigned as the ultimate unit, and search among all kinds of matter revealed about seventy elements, which were duly weighed and classified. The sequence of numbers, which had been devised by the divination of prehistoric instinct, was fitted to the discoveries of the chemist ; and the symmetry of numbers in chemical classifications set new trains of speculation in motion. The cosmos of number revealed blank spaces, and chemists predicted the existence of unknown elements ; ingenious research detected the absentee elements, sometimes in the sun before they were isolated beside us on the earth. But the ultimate atom is now itself undergoing from keen minds a dissection quick and powerful, with instruments sharper than any two-edged sword, piercing even to the dividing asunder of soul and spirit. Like water, the atom is discovered to be an invisible cosmos with terrific potencies. In the act of making such discoveries there is the pure form of high happiness, which always attends the clear perception of truth. Michael Scot, the magician of Fife, inspired by his Arabian teachers at Toledo (1217 A.D.), felt the possibility of such discoveries ; but Dante places him in the nether regions, and his native land made " Auld Michael " responsible for mysterious dangers. The hope of extending the bounds of knowledge is now universal ; and all men rejoice in the achievements of science. But this pleasure is an intellectual luxury and not a spiritual necessity. It was quite possible to live the good life before we knew the nature of air and water. The scientific discoverer also appreciates and honours the good life in himself and others. There arises before the mind of a good man the prospect of new obligations ; the evangelisation of mankind becomes more urgent by reason of man's increasing command of natural forces, and even the evangelisation of the atomic powers themselves calls for serious contemplation.

A League of Nations. The teachers of religion have much to do for the increased welfare of those within their own communities ; and they have to maintain their faithful training of individual character. John Bright is quoted as saying : " I do not believe that all the statesmen in existence, and all the efforts they have ever made, have tended so much to the greatness and true happiness, the purity and glory of this country, as have the efforts of Sunday-school Teachers." But the effect of religious training is to create agreement on the common purposes of great associations. All the prophetic religions desire universal welfare. The disposition they inculcate in half the human race is the only possible presupposition of peace on earth. Success depends upon a sincere desire to avoid war and an active cultivation of the temperament of goodwill. What kind of assistance can prophetic religion offer for the conciliation of nations and of competing social groups ?

There are nearly two thousand millions of people on the earth. Each one has freewill, and self-determination is lately advertised to be a sacred prerogative. What kind of unity is possible among so many free incalculable forces ? Religion has persuaded half the race to accept the Prophets, who bid men to do justly, love mercy, and walk humbly with God. History and geography have limited each man's free choice by dividing men into about a hundred nations ; self-determination cannot change a man's ancestors, language, birthplace, or initial citizenship. Self-preservation becomes the chief end of each nation ; independence, territory, wealth, security become sufficient causes for war. Renunciation of attainable advantage to the detriment of its own citizens is not easy for any State. As the secular result of the biological process, the nation tends to energetic self-assertion.

A modern cause of division appears in the classification of industries. Socialism has absolute dogmas of its own, which limit liberty even more than national boundaries. By organising the production and distribution of man's necessities it is hoped to advance the gains of various classes in each nation. In the view of the Socialist, religion is superstition, or at best a private concern; the supreme good must be attained in this world or not at all. They believe Fichte when he says: " We cannot expect blessedness by the mere fact of our being buried underground." But the whole is greater than the part; and fragments —either national or industrial—each seeking its own advantage, are apt to resort to violence in the vain hope of obtaining it. The causes which create these divisions make forbearance or self-sacrifice a reversal of the natural effect.

Equilibrium among variables in motion is a more subtle problem than balancing constants at rest. If all nations were to maintain their present numbers of population, with equal capacity, diligence, and moral worth, in all time coming, the present distribution of territory might be stereotyped by universal decree. But the tenure of territory has moral conditions; activity, intelligence, chastity exalt a nation, their opposites debase and degrade it. The people of North

America in 1500 A.D. would not have been morally justified in asking mankind to make that Continent a safe place for themselves and their children alone. The moral health of nations is decided by the honour of their homes ; the dictates of international agreements are impotent in this sphere.

To mitigate these secular tendencies to strife, prophetic religion offers certain alleviations. It persuades us so to use our freewill that our aims will harm none and benefit all. It tempers patriotism by including citizens of many nations in a wider spiritual fellowship. The hope of eternal life enables its possessors to accept more easily a temporal disadvantage for the good of others. Among individuals, it generates the hope of reform through penitence. Ordinary experience requires that the impenitent offender must be restrained by his benefactor, by the magistrate, by war, or by excommunication ; but individuals sometimes succeed in reforming character, and magnanimity becomes possible in contemplation to nations. Religion has some-times added intensity to warfare ; but though Churches have deep-seated differences, there is no resort to war any longer. Religion taught States to care for the destitute, to teach children, to free slaves ; no other power can give more

effective aid in teaching men to avoid war.   But
no abstract average of conduct or opinion, no
ethical society can ever displace the Synagogue,
the Church, and the Mosque in the training of
God-fearing men.   Progress towards universal
peace will depend upon loyal adherence to the
spirit and to the organic form of the dialects of
Monotheism.   It is not in the schools of science
and philosophy nor in the assembly of delegates,
but in the Temples of God that the holy fire of
philanthropy can be kept alive.

The end of ungodliness.   The man of to-day asks, Is there
nothing above me that deserves my
respect, my obedience, and my worship ?   There
is a Whole, says the Monist, which consists in
restless matter, infinitely multiplied, unconscious,
blindly generating diversities of existence.   There
is an Absolute, say some philosophers, which
smiles at man as the master of the terrestrial
menagerie, liable to delusions, becoming fanatical
about trifling distinctions like right and wrong.
But such teachers are all agreed that there is
no God, as simple people have so long supposed.
The *Anima Mundi* " sleeps in the mineral,
dreams in the animal, and awakens in man."
The Universe is dumb and inarticulate till it
speaks in its highest production—the human
species.   And among these highest animals,

who shall command the obedience of his kind ? He who has supreme power—the Chief of the State ; *vox imperatoris vox dei.* What this Imperator decrees is right, because he decrees it. He does not hold any commission from Divine Providence ; his authority proceeds from his millions in shining armour. Forthwith follows Armageddon ; and in the fear of God, in abhorrence of war, for the honour of their faith in a God of justice and gentleness, peace-loving men untrained to arms go forth and hardly succeed in disabling the aggressor. "There can only be a strong community where there is agreement in metaphysical convictions," says Troeltsch ; of all things in the welfare of nations a true theism is of unsuspected consequence. By their fruits the systems of philosophy can be known. Men are not aboriginals of the mist and the mud ; the light that is in us is "light from Light," as the Nicene Creed affirms. "The fool hath said in his heart, There is no God. They are corrupt, they have done abominable works" (Ps. 14[1]).

The fruit of the Spirit. What conclusions can we draw from fifty centuries of unforgotten history ? There has been progress in intellect, in character, in general capacity. The progress has not been easy or continuous ; many have despaired of progress, many races have been false to the fountain of life and have disappeared.   The nature of the soul has perplexed and interested all men ; and the response of the soul to ever-acting influences has created religion.   Gifted souls so responded to the influences that surround our life that they dissipated error and proclaimed the sovereign good of human life to be communion with the One Living God.   Such men were called Prophets, and from Amos to Mohammed they agree in acknowledging one Supreme Deity who requires justice and gentleness among men.   To them we owe the sense of moral obligation and the active efforts to promote universal human welfare.

The mental energy of man has in the last century been nobly rewarded by success in the study of natural forces.   The more difficult and subtle task of understanding the human soul has not yet received the same eager attention.   But the forces which created primitive religion are working now ; the communication of one soul with another at a distance, with no material connection, the percipience of what is happening far away, the discovery of water by the divining rod, the faculty of second-sight, the sense of communion with the Blessed Dead, the action of spirit upon spirit in general, are well attested though unexplained elements in real experience. The rare phenomena, which are beyond the normal consciousness—whether above or below —are invitations to examine the inscrutable capacities of the soul. Mother Earth has been travailing for some twenty million years to give each human self the chance of achieving goodness. Every failure is a frustration of the biological process ; every victory not only satisfies biology but gives " joy to the angels in heaven." Marvellous light has rewarded sincere study of things inorganic and sub-human from the molecule to the monkey ; but " the proper study of man-kind is Man." The course of Semitic Religion encourages the lively hope that men will be led into all Truth, and that by loyal obedience to the Light, " which lighteth every man that cometh into the world," they will attain to better health in soul and body.

" For wisdom is more mobile than any motion ;
    Yea, she pervadeth and penetrateth all things by reason
      of her pureness.
  For she is a breath of the power of God,
  And a clear effluence of the glory of the Almighty ;
  Therefore can nothing defiled find entrance into her.
  For she is an effulgence from everlasting light,
  And an unspotted mirror of the working of God,
  And an image of his goodness.
  And she, though but one, hath power to do all things ;
  And remaining in herself, reneweth all things :
  And from generation to generation, passing into holy souls
  She maketh them friends of God, and prophets."
             The Wisdom of Solomon 7[24-27].

INDEX

PRINTED BY MORRISON AND GIBB LIMITED, EDINBURGH

BYWAYS IN EARLY CHRISTIAN LITERATURE:

Studies in the Uncanonical Gospels and Acts.

(The Kerr Lectures.)   **10s.** net.

By the Rev. ADAM FYFE FINDLAY, D.D.

We can never know a country by keeping to the great centres and the high roads. There is need of an introduction in English to a body of literature which is comparatively little known but which has considerable historical value for the study of early Christianity. We are realizing to-day with increasing clearness the extraordinary diversity of thought that was a prominent characteristic of Christianity in the first two centuries.

THE LOCAL COLOUR OF THE BIBLE.

In Three Volumes, each complete in itself.

VOL. I.—GENESIS to II. SAMUEL.   **8s.** net.

  ,, II.—I. KINGS to MALACHI.   *[In preparation*

  ,, III.—THE NEW TESTAMENT.   *[In preparation*

By CHARLES W. BUDDEN, M.D.,

and the Rev. EDWARD HASTINGS, M.A.

Deals with the whole Atmosphere and Background of the Bible—its ideas and language, manners and customs, and the daily life ; religious beliefs and their ritual ; the peculiarities of the country and the influence of the surrounding nations ; the contents of the Bible, history, prophecy, poetry—everything that gives the Bible its own peculiar flavour. Both writers have lived in the East. The one is a student of Science and practical life, the other of History and Religion.

THE LANGUAGE OF PALESTINE AND ADJACENT REGIONS.   **24s.** net.

By the Rev. J. COURTENAY JAMES, B.D.

With Foreword by Sir ERNEST WALLIS BUDGE, Kt.

Sir ERNEST BUDGE says: "I know of no book in which the language of Palestine is similarly treated, and the need for such an introduction to the study of the languages, history, and archæology of Western Asia is very great at the present moment. Its concise and clear diction, and its honest and impartial statements, should render it a peculiarly trustworthy guide to all who take a more than general interest in the Christian East."

THE RELIGIONS OF MODERN SYRIA AND PALESTINE.   7s. net.

By Frederick James Bliss, Ph.D., Rochester, N.Y.

" The work is packed with information. The personal experiences of the author add to the value of a book which all students of Eastern religions will be thankful to have by them."—*Church Times.*

THE GOSPEL HISTORY AND ITS TRANSMISSION.

Third Edition.   Post 8vo.   **12s.** net.

By Professor F. C. Burkitt, D.D., Cambridge.

" Prof. Burkitt has done a great service by this book ; he has imparted a surprising amount of freshness to old themes. His book is delightful reading. It rests on close observation of details vividly conceived ; and yet the selection of points is so admirable, and the touch so light and rapid—never a word wasted, and always, as it would seem, the happiest word chosen—that the reader is carried over subjects that he will be apt to think of as dry and severe with the ease and zest of a romance."—*Expository Times.*

PRIMITIVE CHRISTIANITY AND ITS NON-JEWISH SOURCES.

Authorised Translation.   8vo.   **10s. 6d.** net.

By Professor Carl Clemen, Ph.D., Th.D.

"There is no handbook to the subject in English or German which rivals this comprehensive and serviceable treatise, and its real importance entitles it to the care which the translator has evidently bestowed upon its English dress."

British Weekly.

THE TESTAMENT OF OUR LORD.

Translated into English from the Syriac, with Introduction and Notes.   8vo.   **10s.** net.

By Professor James Cooper, D.D.
and Bishop A. J. Maclean.

"In making the work known, the Editors have done considerable service to the study both of ecclesiastical history and of liturgy. It is a real service, which deserves the gratitude of scholars."—*Guardian.*

BIBLE STUDIES.

Contributions, chiefly from Papyri and Inscriptions, to the History of the Language, Literature, and Religion of Hellenistic Judaism and Primitive Christianity. *Authorised Translation* (incorporating Dr. DEISSMANN's most recent changes and additions). Second Edition. 8vo. **10s.** net.

By Professor C. ADOLPH DEISSMANN, D.D.

"The book so abounds in interesting and important material, bearing on the study of the Bible, that no serious student of the sacred writings can afford to disregard this aid to their understanding. The method of investigation advocated is so far-reaching in its influence that every scholar must take account of it."—*British Weekly*.

HISTORY OF RELIGIONS.

(*International Theological Library.*)

VOL. I. CHINA, JAPAN, EGYPT, BABYLONIA, ASSYRIA, INDIA, PERSIA, GREECE, ROME. **14s.** net.

VOL. II. JUDAISM, CHRISTIANITY, MOHAM-MEDANISM. **14s.** net.

By Professor GEORGE F. MOORE, D.D., LL.D.

"A work whose value and fascination can hardly be imagined by those who only know ' other religions ' through conventional summaries and condensed manuals."—*Christian World*.

MUHAMMAD AND HIS POWER.

(*World's Epoch Makers.*) **4s.** net.

By P. DE LACY JOHNSTONE, M.A.

"This interesting volume gives in a moderate compass a thoroughly good popular account of Muhammad's career and influence. The author is evidently well read in the literature of his subject, and his work could hardly have been better done."—*Guardian*.

HISTORY OF THE JEWISH PEOPLE IN THE TIME OF JESUS CHRIST.

Complete in Five Vols. 8vo. **7s. 6d**. net each ; **37s. 6d.** net.

INDEX VOL. (100 pp. 8vo). **3s. 6d.** net.

By Professor E. SCHÜRER, D.D.

"Every English commentary has for some years contained references to ' Schürer ' as the great authority upon such matters. . . . There is no guide to these intricate and difficult times which even approaches him."—*Record*.

THE BIBLE DOCTRINE OF SOCIETY IN ITS HISTORICAL EVOLUTION.

By the Rev. C. RYDER SMITH, D.D., Richmond.   **18s.** net.

Sociology is at present a subject of pressing importance. This book is the first modern attempt to give a systematic account of Biblical teaching thereon.   The author traces the Evolution of Hebrew Society from Patriarchal times, and outlines its development and progress towards the Final Ideal as contained in the New Testament.   He then examines the principles that this ideal embodies, and discusses the nature of some typical social institutions.

" It is a pleasure to read a book so well written and so well arranged.   Preachers who are thinking men will soon discover that it is alive with stimulus for exposition.   It is most instructive."—Prof. J. MOFFATT.

OLD TESTAMENT HISTORY.

(*International Theological Library.*)   **14s.** net.
By Professor HENRY P. SMITH, D.D., Amherst.

"The history of the little nation out of which was to arise the Sun of Righteousness is clothed with an added charm of actuality, as it is presented in these sane and balanced pages."
Academy.

A HISTORY OF THE CHRISTIAN CHURCH.

In One Volume, 600 pages, with Maps.   **16s.** net.
By Professor WILLISTON WALKER, D.D., Yale.

" The best general history hitherto is now replaced by this volume. . . . A reliable guide to the general study of the subject, and is particularly good in its emphasis on the underlying ideas of the great movements.   Ministers will find it worth having and worth working steadily through, with notebook in hand."—*Baptist Times.*

Edinburgh   T. & T. CLARK   38 George St.